COME 'N' GET IT

Bull trains in front of the Clinton Hotel at Clinton, BC. Supplies for the gold fields, ranches, and stopping houses were hauled over the Cariboo wagon road--an awesome, rough road stretching to the isolated Cariboo and Chilcotin regions, *circa* 1800. GLENBOW ARCHIVES, NA-674-38

BEULAH BARSS

COME 'N' GET IT

★★★ ROUNDUP RECIPES *from* RANCH COUNTRY ★★★

Victoria | Vancouver | Calgary

Previously published in two volumes as *Come 'n Get It: At the Ranch House* (Rocky Mountain Books, 1996) and *Come 'n Get It: Cowboys and Chuckwagons* (Rocky Mountain Books, 1996).

Heritage House Publishing Company Ltd.
heritagehouse.ca

LIBRARY AND ARCHIVES CANADA CATALOGUING IN PUBLICATION

Barss, Beulah M., 1931-, author   Come 'n' get it : roundup recipes from ranch country / Beulah Barss.

Includes index. Previously published: May 1996. Issued in print and electronic formats. ISBN 978-1-77203-125-6 (paperback).—ISBN 978-1-77203-126-3 (epub).—ISBN 978-1-77203-127-0 (pdf)

1. Cooking—Canada, Western. 2. Food habits—Canada, Western—History. 3. Ranch life—Canada, Western—History. 4. Cookbooks. I. Title. II. Title: Come and get it.

TX715.6.B3757 2016   641.59712   C2016-900820-7
C2016-900821-5

Cover design by Jacqui Thomas
Interior book design by Setareh Ashrafologhalai
Interior illustrations by Setareh Ashrafologhalai
Cover photos: Glenbow Archives, NA-207-72 (*front*), and Glenbow Archives, NB-H16-452 (*back*)

The interior of this book was produced on 100% post-consumer recycled paper, processed chlorine free and printed with vegetable-based inks.

We acknowledge the financial support of the Government of Canada through the Canada Book Fund and the Canada Council for the Arts, and the Province of British Columbia through the British Columbia Arts Council and the Book Publishing Tax Credit.

20 19 18 17 16   1 2 3 4 5

Printed in Canada

 CONTENTS

≋ INTRODUCTION ≋

COME 'N' GET IT celebrates the early days of cattle ranching in western Canada. Whether in a chuckwagon on the range or in the ranch-house kitchen, the people who prepared meals for hungry cowboys, ranch hands, family, and friends were a hardy bunch who knew how to make the most of what they had. This book pays tribute not only to the food of the early times, but to the lifestyle and wonderful hospitality of the ranching community.

Cattle ranching in British Columbia had its beginning in the Cariboo gold rush. The miners who struggled into that rugged and remote area were prepared to put up with great hardships, but they drew the line at a steady diet of beans. They wanted meat.

A Lazy Susan on a table in Burns Ranch House. HERITAGE PARK, CALGARY, ALBERTA

A few enterprising men organized cattle drives, with up to five hundred head at a time, from the western United States to the Cariboo. There the animals were quickly sold for a profit. When gold petered out, the remaining cattle formed the nucleus of some of the great cattle ranches of today.

The North West Mounted Police set the stage for ranching in Alberta and Saskatchewan. They provided a market for beef and developed a peaceful relationship with the First Nations. Grazing leases were cheap, and ranchers could turn cattle out on the open range to feed on the nourishing prairie grasses. Powerful ranches were formed: the Cochrane, the Bar U, Oxley, Walrond, Matador, and others.

Food supplies were transported over great distances and had to be stored for weeks and months. The supply list was simple: flour, sugar, coffee, beans, rice, oatmeal, dried fruits, canned tomatoes, molasses, corn syrup, yeast cakes, baking soda, salt, and a few spices.

A typical diet for a small ranch without a cook was "plenty of hot biscuits, fried salt pork, beans or rice, stewed prunes for dessert and lots of corn syrup."

The correct riding attire—a jacket, skirt or trousers, boots, gloves, and hat. At the turn of the century, "ladies" rode sidesaddle, both legs on the same side of the English-style saddle.
GLENBOW ARCHIVES, NC-39-241

If large, the ranch employed a cook, whose job was to feed the ranch hands. The cook at the Bar U went out of his way to look after the boys. Every Sunday morning he left the house with his willow pole and bits of red fabric to tie onto a fishing hook. He waded into Pekisko Creek and threw in his line once for each man that he had to feed. It is said he never missed and that every Sunday morning there was a fish fry in the cookhouse.

In the early days the cooks were men, but as more women came West, they eventually took over the task. As the character and size of

A cowboy finds a quiet place for a meal durning a cattle round up, *circa* 1920.

ranches changed, so did the method of working. Women were expected to participate in the running of the ranch, as were the children. Ranchers butchered their own animals, corned beef, ground sausages, smoked bacon, saved drippings for cooking or making soap, preserved fruit, and prepared jam. Large gardens produced vegetables for canning, pickling, and storing in the root cellar. Bread, buns, pies, and cakes were baked at home.

During the devastating cold winter of 1906–07, thousands of cattle froze to death, bringing economic disaster to the owners. The completion of the railroad brought settlers wanting farmland and barbed-wire fences. A new generation of ranchers emerged, usually with less money and land but with more experience and a different style of ranching. However, that part of the ranching story is for others to tell.

Generally, ranch people were thrifty and self-reliant. They were proud of their ability to produce and prepare food from their land. They remain so today.

Ranching no longer dominates the Canadian West, but it remains an important industry. Its traditions of simple, gracious living, love of the outdoors, and a spirit of freedom and adventure are revered today. And an appetite for old-fashioned ranch foods remains hearty.

The recipes and stories for this book were collected from letters, diaries, manuscripts, history books, family cookbooks, and personal interviews with ranching families. There have been many enjoyable occasions and extraordinary instances of hospitality offered during my research: an invitation sight unseen by the Osbornes to their lovely ranch home nestled near old Fort Walsh; a viewing of Laura Parsonage's private collection of pioneer-ranch-house artifacts; dinner with Dorothy Blades on an old-fashioned ranch table with a swinging Lazy Susan centre; a day with Bert Sheppard at the OH Ranch and an invitation to his eightieth-birthday party; a visit with Meriel Hayden; lunch and pemmican at Jean Hoare's and a view of Willow Creek, where the bull trains camped overnight a hundred years ago; Fred McKinnon's introduction to his fabulous family; a visit to the Commercial Hotel in Maple Creek; a fall drive through the beautiful Cariboo country.

My sincere thanks to all who provided information and to the helpful staff of the many museums and archives that I visited.

SOUPS ★ AND ★ SALADS

⚛ BEEF AND BARLEY SOUP ⚛

2½ lbs (1 kg) beef shin bones
    with some meat on them
bacon drippings or beef fat
2 onions, sliced
½ cup (125 mL) barley
10 cups (2.5 L) water
1 tbsp (15 mL) salt
2 beef bouillon cubes (optional)

In the late 1800s, Harry "Kamoose" Taylor ran a hotel in Fort Macleod that became a gathering place for cattlemen. One rather stately gentleman from the Oxley Ranch inquired as to what type of soup would be served for dinner. "Damned good soup" came the reply. It was probably beef and barley soup.

SELECT A HEAVY pot with a tightly fitting lid. Brown the beef bones in the fat. Brown the sliced onions. Add the barley and water and simmer, or bake in a 300°F (150°C) oven for 4 hours.

Remove the meat and bone, cut the meat into large bite-sized pieces, and return to the soup. Add salt. If necessary, add 2 dissolved beef bouillon cubes.

 ★ EARLY RANCH HOMES ★

EARLY RANCH HOMES were simple affairs. The first accommodation was often a tent on the ground. In parts of Saskatchewan and Alberta where there were few if any trees, the ranchers lived in sod dwellings made by piling blocks of heavy prairie sod over a log frame. As soon as possible, log structures were built, usually low two- or three-room houses with one door leading outdoors and a window on each side. Along the Whitemud River in Saskatchewan, the log homes were whitewashed with local clay. But in most areas the exterior logs were left to weather with no finish.

Many interiors were given a light coat of calcimine, which brightened them considerably. In other homes, the walls and ceilings were covered with coarse white cotton, which made the interior warmer and brighter. Other interiors were papered with old newspapers to keep out winter drafts.

The log home of the Macleod family in Alberta was well papered with old newspapers during the visit of Lord Lorne. When he remained on his knees long after everyone else had risen from morning prayers, the Macleods were quite impressed with Lord Lorne's devoutness, until they realized he was merely reading an article on the wall.

≋ THREE BEAN SALAD ≋

MAKE THIS SALAD the day before you plan to serve it. Drain beans well and combine with the sliced onions and mushrooms. Shake oil, vinegar, sugar, salt, and pepper in a jar. Pour over the bean mixture. Cover and refrigerate, stirring occasionally.

Just before serving, drain beans and pile on crisp salad greens or toss with an equal portion of greens using a little bit of marinade as a dressing.

14-oz (398 mL) can cut wax beans

14-oz (398 mL) can French-style green beans

14-oz (398 mL) can kidney beans

1 can mushrooms (optional)

1 cup (250 mL) thinly sliced onions

½ cup (125 mL) salad oil

½ cup (125 mL) dark cider vinegar

¾ cup (175 mL) sugar

salt and pepper to taste

Serves 8

≋ COLESLAW ≋

Coleslaw has always been part of the western food tradition. This recipe makes a coleslaw that is crunchier than most.

IN A JAR, shake together vinegar, oil, sugar, and salt. Add to cabbage and mix. Refrigerate for several hours.

2 tbsp (30 mL) vinegar

½ cup (125 mL) vegetable oil

3 tbsp (45 mL) sugar

½ tsp (2 mL) salt

½ head cabbage, shredded to make 4 cups

Serves 4 to 5

TOMATO ASPIC

14-oz (398 mL) can canned tomatoes

½ cup (125 mL) water

3-oz (85 g) package lemon Jell-O
      powder

1 tbsp (15 mL) vinegar

dash of Worcestershire sauce

Serves 4 to 6

Tomato aspic is a good accompaniment for spiced beef at winter buffets and makes a refreshing jellied salad for cold suppers.

BRING TOMATOES and water to a boil; stir in remaining ingredients. (Do not break up tomatoes.) Cool slightly and pour into a glass serving bowl. Serve cold.

★ PASS THE HONEY ★

WHEN AN UNATTACHED female came west to pay a visit to friends and relatives, it was necessary to build an extra hitching post to hold the visitors' horses. It wasn't long before one of the bachelors, tired of his own cooking and his lonely shack, wooed her into becoming his bride.

Some of the bachelors managed their households very well, while others with a limited knowledge of the household arts contributed a great deal to the general amusement of their neighbours. A visitor at such an Alberta ranch was surprised during supper when his host brought out a keg of honey and rolled it along behind the chairs for each person to help himself. The visitor asked if it might be more convenient to put some honey into a bowl and pass it around. Such a procedure had never occurred to his host.

Porridge, prunes, and potatoes were reputed to be cooked in the same pot without a rinse in the dishpan. Shirts were washed in the nearest creek and hung over a rock to dry. Pants were worn for such a long time that when taken off, they stood up on their own.

However, the ultimate in casual housekeeping occurred in the bachelor shack of Ashe, Cotter, and de Rinzy. Rather than carry their ashes outside, they left them on the dirt floor of their cabin until a good-sized pile was collected, at which time they hitched a team of oxen to the cabin and moved it to a new site.

From the papers of John D. Higinbotham (Glenbow Archives)

MEATS ★ AND ★ POULTRY

BEEFSTEAK AND KIDNEY PIE

4 tbsp (60 mL) beef fat or lard

4 lbs (2 kg) blade or chuck steak,
   cut into 1-inch (2.5 cm) pieces

½ to ¾ lbs (250 to 375 g) lamb or
   beef kidney

2 medium onions, minced

⅔ cup (150 mL) flour

2 tsp (10 mL) salt

½ tsp (2 mL) freshly ground pepper

4 cups (1 L) beef broth (canned or
   made with beef bouillon cubes)

2 tsp (10 mL) prepared mustard

1½ tbsp (20 mL) Worcestershire
   sauce

½ tsp (2 mL) cinnamon

1 tsp (5 mL) ginger

2 cups (500 mL) mushrooms,
   sliced (optional)

pie pastry for topping

_____

Serves 8 to 10

MELT FAT IN a Dutch oven; brown beef and kidney. Add onion and sauté. Mix flour, salt, and pepper. Sprinkle over meat and stir. Add beef broth, mustard, Worcestershire sauce, cinnamon, and ginger. Cover and simmer over low heat until tender, about 2½ hours, or bake in a 300°F (150°C) oven until tender. Add mushrooms, if using. If the liquid is too thin, thicken with flour mixed to a paste with water. If too thick, thin with red wine or water. Grease a 9 × 13 inch (23 × 33 cm) baking dish. Add the meat and liquid. Cool.

While the meat is cooling, prepare the pie pastry (see page 78). Place pastry over meat, moistening and pinching to the edge of the dish. Make vents in the pastry to allow steam to escape. Bake in hot oven, 450°F (230°C), for 10 minutes. Lower temperature to 375°F (190°C) and continue baking for 15 minutes or until the pie crust is golden brown.

★ SPIN 'ER AND GRAB ★

THAT'S WHAT YOU did at the big, round, ranch-style table designed to serve busy cowhands on the run. In the centre was a pine-covered wagon wheel, lying flat on its axis. This held the platter of sliced beef; the bowls of potatoes, gravy, and turnips; a plate of bread; two or three raisin pies; a jug of condensed milk; and an enamel pot of steaming coffee. On the top of the hub rested a coal-oil lamp. On the large circular lower level sat the plates, cups, knives, and forks. Around the table sat the cowboys, ten easily, but more could be crowded in if necessary. A flick of the finger rotated the inner wheel and brought within easy serving the salt, syrup, or whichever other item the diner fancied.

Fred Anderson of the Oxley Ranch is credited with building Canada's first spinning table. It soon became popular in many bunkhouse kitchens. Cowhands would drift in for their meal when their work was finished, find an empty place, and turn the wheel to bring the dinner to them. That way, a cook could serve many hands quickly and smoothly.

≋ BOILED BEEF WITH ≋ HORSERADISH SAUCE

Ranchers lived off their land, and when they butchered their own meat, they used every part of the animal. Joan Boyd of Longview, Alberta, suggested including this recipe for boiled beef, a dish that can be prepared from the shank, neck, and other tough but flavourful meat cuts. It was served on a large platter, bones included. The bone marrow was, and still is, considered a treat.

PLACE THE BEEF in a pot and just cover with water. Simmer for 3 to 4 hours or until almost tender. Add onions, carrots, salt, and pepper, and simmer for 45 minutes. Save the beef broth for making vegetable soup. Serve with horseradish sauce and boiled potatoes.

HORSERADISH SAUCE

IN A SAUCEPAN, melt the butter and stir in the flour. Add milk and stir over medium heat until thick. Add salt, pepper, and grated horseradish. Serve cold.

4 lbs (2 kg) boiling beef

small onions, 1 to 1½ per person

4 carrots, quartered

1 tsp (5 mL) salt

pepper to taste

HORSERADISH SAUCE

2 tbsp (30 mL) butter

2 tbsp (30 mL) flour

1 cup (250 mL) milk

½ tsp (2 mL) salt

pepper to taste

¼ cup (50 mL) grated
    horseradish

≋ CORNED BEEF ≋

5 lbs (2.5 kg) beef brisket

8 cups (2 L) water

¾ cup (175 mL) coarse or pickling salt

½ tbsp (7 mL) saltpetre (purchased
　　at drugstore)

¼ cup (50 mL) brown sugar

1 tbsp (15 mL) mixed pickling spice

½ tsp (2 mL) onion salt

¼ tsp (1 mL) garlic powder

1 bay leaf

Corned beef is beef that has been pickled in a salt solution or dry salt mixture and then given a long, slow cooking. This recipe will make a delicious home-cured corned beef that keeps well in the refrigerator and can be sliced for sandwiches when needed.

CORNING

Prepare the brine by boiling the water, salt, saltpetre, sugar, and spices for 5 minutes. Cool. Place the brisket in a crock or bowl (not metal). Cover with the brine. The meat will float, so place a plate on top to keep it immersed. Cover and leave in a cool place for at least 14 days before cooking. Turn the meat every few days. Should the brine become thick or ropy, wash the meat in cold water, wash the crock, and replace the old brine with a fresh brine.

COOKING

Rinse the corned beef. Place in a pot and cover with cold water. Bring to a boil and remove the scum that collects on top. Cover the pot and simmer for 4 to 5 hours or until tender. If you wish, add vegetables to the liquid about 30 minutes before meat is done. Serve hot or cold. When cooling, place a heavy plate on top of the meat. This will flatten it and make slicing easier.

★ COWBOY DRESS ★

JOHN HAWKES DESCRIBED the utility of cowboy garb In *The Story of Saskatchewan and Its People, Vol. 2* (S.J. Clarke, Chicago, 1924). Far from being merely ornamental, cowboy clothes and equipment were functional and indispensable. Hardly a thing worn or used was not absolutely necessary.

The big handkerchief worn around the neck was pulled up to cover the nose and mouth when the dust from a thousand moving steers made breathing difficult. The handkerchief was knotted behind the neck, leaving the wide part free in front, ready when needed with no unnecessary fumbling.

If a whirling lasso were to run over a roper's arm, it could cut to the bone. To protect himself, the cowboy wore gloves on his hands and heavy leather cuffs on his wrists.

His broad-brimmed hat kept off the scorching sun of summer and sheltered him from rain during wet weather. It was held on by a string; without it, the wind would have blown the hat off and under the feet of the cattle.

The high-heeled boots were a necessity. They kept the rider's feet from slipping through the stirrups when a horse was bucking and often saved him from being caught in the stirrups and possibly dragged to death when thrown. The cowboy wore leather chaps over his pants to protect his legs when riding through thorns and brush. They also shielded him from wind, rain, flies, and mosquitoes.

Charlie Millar, a famous rider and roper who broke broncos for the Bar U Ranch at High River. He was fast with his six-shooter, played the mouth organ, and wrote poetry.

GLENBOW ARCHIVES, NA-466-14

He carried a bullwhip. In a herd of cattle, there were always a few mean ones that would, on the slightest provocation, start a stampede. One end of the bullwhip was loaded, and when the rider saw trouble brewing, he spotted the bad steer, rode up, and gave it the weight of the butt end of the whip, which usually made the steer behave. The lash was for clipping tardy ones on the nose to hurry them up and to remind any that might stray from the herd that their place was with the bunch.

Of course, the cowboy had a good saddle. As he lived in the saddle, he wanted it as comfortable as possible, made of fine leather and with a solid frame. The seat had to be strong, and the horn strong enough that the horse could put all its weight on a rope tied to the horn when holding or hauling a steer.

A fine bridle was part of the cowboy's gear. Plaited hair for special occasions was popular, and some put as much as one hundred dollars into a bridle alone. Spurs were sometimes silver plated, but what of it? These things were part of the working equipment of the cowpuncher, and it made sense to have the very best.

⚛ CORNED BEEF HASH ⚛

2 cups (500 mL) cooked potatoes,
    finely diced

12-oz (340 g) can corned beef

1 medium onion, finely chopped

2 tsp (10 mL) prepared mustard
    freshly ground pepper to taste

Chunks of beef were corned or pickled in a salt solution to keep them fresh during warm summer months. The corned beef was boiled and served with vegetables or baked and covered with a brown-sugar glaze. Leftovers were chopped and made into hash for a delicious, simple supper.

MIX POTATOES, corned beef, onion, mustard, and pepper. Fry in butter until crispy on both sides.

≋ PRAIRIE OYSTERS ≋ (CALVES' FRIES)

Once a year, generally in early summer, the spring calves are brought in for branding. The testicles of bull calves are removed so they can grow into marketable steer beef. At many brandings, it is customary to serve the testicles for a snack or for supper. When prepared, they are known as "prairie oysters" or "calves' fries."

calves' testicles

pail of salted water

1 egg, beaten

¼ cup (50 mL) milk cracker crumbs

butter or beef fat for frying

salt and pepper to taste

AFTER THE TESTICLES have been removed, soak them in a pail of salted water. For a 4-gallon (16 L) pail of water, use 1 cup (250 mL) of salt. Before cooking, remove any excess tubing and connective tissue and rinse with clean water. Combine the egg and milk. Dip the testicles in the egg-milk mixture, then roll in the cracker crumbs.

Melt butter or fat, enough to give ½ inch (1.5 cm) of hot fat, in a frying pan. Fry the testicles in hot fat. Serve from the pan with salt and pepper.

⫸ RANCH HOUSE MEAT LOAF ⫷

2 lbs (1 kg) ground beef

½ cup (125 mL) finely chopped onion

1 cup (250 mL) bread or cracker
  crumbs

2 eggs

¾ of 10-oz (284 mL) can
  beef broth

1 tsp (5 mL) salt

1 tsp (5 mL) parsley

1 tsp (5 mL) sage

1 tsp (5 mL) thyme

¼ tsp (1 mL) pepper

TOPPING

3 tbsp (45 mL) brown sugar

4 tbsp (60 mL) ketchup

1 tsp (5 mL) dry mustard

Serves 6

The aroma of meat loaf wafting from a ranch kitchen is ambrosia to a hungry cowhand.

MIX ALL THE ingredients together. Pack into a 5 × 9 inch (13 × 23 cm) loaf pan. Bake at 325°F (160°C) for 75 minutes. Remove from oven after 45 minutes, brush with topping (ingredients should be mixed together), and bake for another 30 minutes. Turn out of pan and place on an oven-proof serving dish.

★ THE ROUNDUP ★

THE ROUNDUP WAS the gathering of cattle from the open range in Saskatchewan and southern Alberta. It was the most characteristic institution of the early range, and the most picturesque, with the herds of cattle and horses, the wagons, and open cooking fires. At first, a large general roundup was held. When this proved impractical, smaller roundups were organized in various well-marked natural districts.

During winter the cattle drifted in widely separated areas as they fed. Sometimes they scattered during severe storms. Spring roundups were organized to locate and gather them together. In the early years the cattle were branded right there, on the open range, and turned loose immediately. In later years they were driven to the ranches of their respective owners for branding. The roundup began about May 24. Stockmen and riders from all parts of the range joined together, selected a captain, loaded the chuckwagon and gear, gathered the horses, and pulled out. There might be five or six outfits in all, each with a cook and tents sufficient to accommodate all hands.

Each cowboy had a string of six or more horses. As he could ride only one at a time, the others were kept in a rope corral, tended during the day by the "day wrangler" and through the night by the "nighthawk."

The first chore in the morning, after pulling on clothes and packing up the bedroll, was to select and rope a horse for the morning's work. The roundup captain gave instructions and directed the cowboys in

Roundup at Cochrane Lake, Alberta, *circa* 1905. GLENBOW ARCHIVES, NA-2365-34

their search for cattle. Horses and riders fanned out across the country, making large circles with a radius of five to ten miles. The cattle were herded back to the camp and held there in a large milling herd.

After a hot meal at midday, the cowboys chose well-trained, older horses for the afternoon work of cutting herd. When the sharp-eyed riders spied an animal with their ranch brand, they signalled their horses to go after it. It was "worked" to the edge of the herd, where waiting cowboys moved it to one of several groups, according to its brand.

The same routine was carried on until the entire area had been ridden, the calves all branded, and the cattle placed on their respective ranges.

There were other roundups organized in a similar manner: fall roundups to brand animals missed in the spring, beef roundups to select animals for market, and horse roundups to gather horses that were to be broken, branded, or sold.

A bunkhouse interior reflecting the simple needs of the western cowboy: a potbellied stove, beds, and a few pieces of furniture, *circa* 1894. GLENBOW ARCHIVES, NA-237-15

★ A FELLER NEVER RAPPED ★

HOSPITALITY IN THE WEST went beyond politeness and charitableness. There was a general understanding, an unwritten rule, that a man be accepted for what he was and be made welcome at the ranch. "A feller never rapped," Frank Gallup of Longview, Alberta, told me in an interview in 1980. "He just put his horse in the corral, fed him, slackened the cinch, then came into the house and said, 'God damn it, I haven't eaten for a week!' and you fed him and he would spend the night. You never asked questions of where he was going or where he had been. Every man minded his own affairs but helped another too."

If a visitor stopped by and found the ranch house empty, he just went inside and made a meal anyway. Many times a rancher and his wife would return from an outing to find the dishes washed and the cups turned upside down on the saucers, an indication that a visitor had been there and had made himself at home.

⚜ RANCH HOUSE STEW ⚜

If serving this dish to guests, prepare stew ahead of time and have ingredients measured for the biscuit topping. The dish will then take only a few minutes to assemble.

BEEF-STEW BASE

Trim fat from meat. Render the fat in a heavy pan; discard the dried bits. Brown meat in rendered fat (add lard if there is not enough). Remove meat and brown onions. Return the meat to the pan. Add flour and paprika. Stir well. Continue cooking for a few minutes.

Add the tomatoes, beer, Worcestershire sauce, stock, bay leaves, parsley, and thyme. Cover and bake in a 300°F (150°C) oven or simmer on top of stove for 3 hours, until meat is tender. Add mushrooms, salt, and pepper.

Pour stew into a 3-quart (3 L) casserole (or two smaller casseroles). Prepare the biscuit crust (recipe below). Cut dough to fit the size of the casserole(s). Place over stew and seal edges tightly to keep flavour in. Brush the top with milk and bake in a 400°F (200°C) oven for approximately 20 minutes or until browned.

BISCUIT CRUST

Mix dry ingredients. Work in butter until mixture resembles crumbs. Beat egg with the milk. Make a well in centre of dry ingredients; pour in egg and milk and mix until one lump of dough is obtained. Roll out on a floured board to ½-inch (1.5 cm) thickness.

BEEF-STEW BASE

4 lbs (2 kg) beef rump or stewing
   meat, cut into cubes

4 large onions, chopped

¾ cup (175 mL) flour

1 tsp (5 mL) paprika

1 cup (250 mL) canned tomatoes

1 glass beer (optional)

2 tsp (10 mL) Worcestershire sauce

4 cups (1 L) brown stock or water
   with 4 beef bouillon cubes
   dissolved

3 bay leaves

1 tsp (5 mL) parsley

¼ tsp (1 mL) thyme

2 cups (500 mL) mushrooms,
   whole or sliced

1 tsp (5 mL) salt

pepper to taste

BISCUIT CRUST

2 cups (500 mL) flour

1 tbsp (15 mL) baking powder

½ tsp (2 mL) salt

4 tbsp (60 mL) butter

1 egg

¾ cup (175 mL) milk

Serves 8 to 10

⚛ WAGON STEW ⚛

2 lbs (1 kg) stewing meat, lean
  short ribs, or chuck

2 tbsp (30 mL) beef fat or lard

4 tbsp (60 mL) flour

2 medium onions, sliced

2½ cups (625 mL) water

1 cup (250 mL) canned tomatoes

1 tbsp (15 mL) chili powder

1-2 beef bouillon cubes

1 tsp (5 mL) salt pepper to taste

vegetables if desired*

_____

Serves 5 to 6

This full-bodied, delicious stew satisfies appetites made keen by hard work and fresh air. It is one variation of the many stews served on chuckwagons in the early West.

CUT THE MEAT into 1-inch (2 cm) cubes. Melt the beef fat or lard in a heavy pan or Dutch oven with a tightly fitting lid. If using beef fat, discard the bits of residue. Add the meat and brown. Sprinkle the flour over the meat and toss lightly. Add the onions, water, tomatoes, chili powder, beef bouillon cubes, salt, and pepper. Cover and bake in 300°F (150°C) oven or simmer on top of the stove for approximately 3½ hours or until tender.

* Cut vegetables such as carrots, parsnips, turnips, and potatoes into chunks and add during the last hour of cooking. Add fresh or frozen green peas during the last 5 minutes. The stew is also good served with vegetables such as mashed potatoes on the side.

★ THE CHUCKWAGON ★

THE CHUCKWAGON was kitchen, dining room, social centre, and home to cowboys moving a herd of cattle or riding in a roundup.

It was really a light mountain wagon with high wheels and strong wide-gauged axles strengthened to withstand wild rides over rough country. The bottom sideboards were of wood. Wooden bows, over which a canvas sheet was pulled for protection on rainy days, were arched over the top. A large mess box built of strong lumber was placed upright at the back of the wagon and held in place by steel rods running across the wagon and through the box. Fitted with shelves and drawers, the box made a convenient cupboard. Its hinged door was let down to rest on a wooden support and formed a work table for the cook.

It was the cook's duty to prepare the chuckwagon for spring work. He scrubbed the cupboards with boiling water and lye soap. Pots, frying pans, and eating utensils were scoured with soap and sand. The water barrel was cleaned and soaked to swell its seams so there would be no possibility of leakage. The axles were greased, the harness mended, and the horses broken.

Then the wagon was packed with enough provisions to feed sixteen to twenty men for several weeks at a time. Salt, sugar, tea, and coffee were stored in pails with tightly fitting lids. Sacks of flour and beans, cases of dried fruit, cans of milk, and a case of canned tomatoes were placed in the bed of the wagon. Tin plates and cups and cooking and eating utensils were packed in the mess-box compartments. The heavy cooking pots were stored at the bottom. Empty flour sacks, carefully washed and folded, were pushed into a corner to be used for towels and aprons. The stove was attached to one side of the wagon, a water barrel to the other. Sometimes the bedrolls, ropes, and extra gear were thrown on too; however, during a large roundup, a separate wagon carried equipment other than food.

When the wagon was ready to roll, the cook hitched up the team, climbed up to the driver's seat and took off across the unsettled land.

Bar U Ranch on Pekisko Creek near Longview, Alberta, *circa* 1892. They are arranged on both sides of the roadway like streets of a small village. The old log buildings are fine examples of pioneer ranch construction. GLENBOW ARCHIVES, NA-466-12

★ THE BAR U ★

THE RIVER LEAVES the foot of the high bluffs and takes a sweep north, then turns east once more. The bend forms a cozy corner of level land a mile long and nearly one hundred yards wide. High bluffs and heavy bush on either side of the stream afford excellent shelter to the north.

At the western end stood the manager's house, with its long, straggling line of outbuildings. East were the breaking stables and corrals, the team stables, wagon sheds, and men's quarters—all built in a straight line along the north side of the trail that passes through the ranch. Opposite this were several log shanties used as storehouses, giving the whole the appearance of a little village street. The branding corrals were on the hill north of where the trail dips into the valley, and the feeding corral stood on the bottom on the other side of the river.

This was the Bar U Ranch in the Pekisko Creek valley, second oldest of the Alberta ranches and one of the most successful. In the early 1900s, forty thousand cattle carried its brand. When horses were an important source of power, there were over four hundred purebred Percheron mares, the largest herd in the world. There were also fine saddle horses, bred from thoroughbred stallions.

The Bar U was always well managed and well run. It was called the training ground for cattlemen, as many of the noted stockmen of the West were associated with it at some time: Fred Stimson, Bill Moodie, John Ware, George Lane, Herb Millar, Joe Brown, Pat Burns, Charlie McKinnon, and many others.

≋ RANCH-STYLE STEAK ≋

Beefsteak on the Bar U ranch was usually round steak—tenderized, floured, spiced, and fried in beef fat. This cooking method produced a delicious steak that is still a favourite today. Shirley Merle Osborne served delicious ranch-style steak during a visit in 1981.

TRIM THE FAT off the steak and put it into a heavy kettle or Dutch oven over high heat to render the fat. If there is not a good layer of fat in the bottom of the kettle, add a piece of lard. Cut the steak into serving portions and pound each piece on both sides with the edge of a saucer, hard enough to break almost through the meat.

Smear each piece with mustard, sprinkle with salt and pepper, roll and pound in flour. Cook the pieces quickly in hot fat until they are golden brown on each side. When done, pile them on a platter and keep them warm in the oven until serving time. Gravy can be made from the bits and pieces in the kettle by adding flour and water, or flour and a can of mushroom soup and water.

2 lbs (1 kg) round steak*

prepared mustard

salt and pepper

flour

Serves 4 to 5

* If you would prefer, buy minute steaks or cube steaks, or have the butcher pass your round steak through a tenderizer. Flatten the steak and apply flour and mustard, then cook as above.

⇛ SAUSAGE ROLLS ⇚

ROUGH PUFF PASTRY

2 cups (500 mL) flour

¼ tsp (1 mL) salt

¾ cup (175 mL) butter, very
  cold and hard (or ½ cup/
  125 mL butter and ¼ cup/
  50 mL lard)

3 to 4 tbsp (45 to 60 mL) cold
  water to mix

½ tsp (2 mL) lemon juice

MEAT FILLING

Combine:

1 lb (500 g) sausage meat

1 small onion, grated (about
  2 tbsp or 30 mL)

1 tbsp (15 mL) chopped parsley

salt and pepper to taste

Makes approximately eighteen 2-inch (5 cm) rolls or thirty-six 1-inch (2.5 cm) rolls

Millarville, Alberta, was named after early settlers, the Malcolm Millars, who ran the first post office in the area. In correspondence with me, Mildred McMillan recalled that Mrs. Millar frequently made sausage rolls, as did many other ranch women in the area. They were part of picnic lunches taken to the Millarville Races.

SIFT THE FLOUR and salt together. Cut in the fat, leaving it in small pieces. Make a well in the centre. Add the lemon juice and just enough of the water to make a stiff dough. Refrigerate about 1 hour before using.

ASSEMBLING THE SAUSAGE ROLLS

Cut the pastry in half. Roll half of the pastry into a 9 × 13-inch (23 × 33 cm) rectangle. Form one half of the sausage meat into 3 rolls the length of the pastry and place on the pastry, spaced an equal distance apart. Cut the pastry into strips wide enough to encircle the meat. Dampen one edge of each strip, fold over, and press together firmly. Cut into rolls of desired length. Make a slash on top of each roll. Repeat with the other half of the pastry and sausage. Brush the tops with a small amount of beaten egg yolk. Place on a baking sheet with a raised edge. Bake in a hot oven (425°F/220°C) for approximately 20 to 30 minutes.

★ HORSE RACING AND HUNTING ★

RANCHERS HAD A passion for horse racing, whether it was an informal race between two cowboys showing off their favourite horses or an organized event with competitors from across the country. Almost every village and town had a racing track of some sort, and there were tracks even where there were no towns. According to Frank Gallup, everyone participated, cowboys and ranchers.

The Mitford and Cochrane Annual Race was a full-day affair with twenty-one events. The most prestigious, the Gentleman Ranchers' Race, called for a race of one mile. The requirements were that the horse had been owned by its master for at least three months prior to the race and that it had never been ridden in the racing circuit.

Families arrived in buggies, wagons, and democrats. Old friends were reunited, and everyone talked horses. At noon, tablecloths were spread on the ground and picnic lunches brought out. One glimpsed roast chicken, basins of salad, sausage rolls, meat patties, sandwiches, fudge layer cake, jelly rolls, cookies, and doughnuts.

A gathering at the Davies ranch, Crawling Valley, Alberta, *circa* 1909. GLENBOW ARCHIVES, NA-2142-2

At the turn of the century, ranchers of British origin raised hounds and organized hunts similar to the traditional fox hunts in the old country. Both men and women participated, making quite a sight as they galloped across the prairies after the lowly coyote. As well as providing sport, the hunts helped keep the coyote population in check.

After the fall roundup, many ranchers loaded up pack strings and rode into the hills for a week or two of big-game hunting. In an interview with me in Okotoks, Alberta, in 1977, Mary Dover recalled that her grandfather, a rancher and former colonel in the North West Mounted Police, always looked forward to a fall hunt in the foothills and always took with him a meat pie made in a metal wash basin and large enough to provide a meal for several days.

≋ SPICED BEEF ≋

12 to 14 lbs (6 to 7 kg) rolled round of beef

1 cup (250 mL) brown sugar

1½ cups (375 mL) coarse or pickling salt

3 tbsp (45 mL) allspice

3 tbsp (45 mL) cloves

2 tbsp (30 mL) saltpetre

½ cup (125 mL) peppercorns (cracked)

When the Cowans lived on the Onward Ranch in British Columbia, it was traditional to serve spiced beef at an open house during Christmas week. "It always caused a little sensation," recalled Vivian Cowan in her letters to friend Fay Hartt. The original recipe specified a whole round of beef, with the bone removed and the cavity filled with suet, tied up and marinated in spices for three weeks.

TO MARINATE THE MEAT

Tie beef with heavy cord to hold its shape. Rub brown sugar into meat on all sides, place meat in a bowl or crock, and leave in a cool place for 3 days.* Once a day, rub meat with sugar liquid and turn.

After the beef has marinated in the sugar liquid for 3 days, mix together salt, allspice, cloves, saltpetre, and peppercorns. Rub into beef and return to the bowl or crock. Store in a cool place for 2 to 3 weeks. Each day, turn meat to opposite side and rub all sides with the collected juices.

* If you do not have a suitable crock, place marinated meat in a large zip-lock plastic bag (double-bag to be sure it won't leak). Store in the back of the refrigerator and turn every day.

TO COOK THE MEAT

Drain meat and wrap tightly in foil. Bake in a 300°F (150°C) oven for approximately 2 to 3 hours. Use a meat thermometer, and cook to medium rare or your preference. Cool in its juices and store in the refrigerator.

To serve, carve across grain in very thin slices. Serve with tomato aspic, two or three varieties of sliced buttered bread, mustard, and horseradish.

A happy group enjoying a sleigh ride on Rosebud Creek, Alberta. GLENBOW ARCHIVES, NC-43-67

★ CHRISTMAS ON THE RANCH ★

WHEN IT'S -32°F outside, the house is snug within. The Christmas tree, strung with threaded cranberries, lends a festive air, while the tissue-wrapped presents heighten the feeling of expectancy.

In correspondence housed at the BC Archives, Vivian Cowan, of the Onward Ranch at 150 Mile House, British Columbia, described Christmas on the ranch:

"We always have to wait Christmas morning until the cattle are fed, hundreds of them and of course being so cold it takes longer to do as they get extra then so it's about eleven when Hugh comes in and gives his men a hot rum. He then changes to be ready for the fray. Meanwhile the children are almost bursting with impatience. Finally we all gather.

"The presents are opened. Friends drop by. Dinner preparations are made and the smell of turkey permeates the house. The long table is covered with an Irish linen tablecloth, candles and Christmas crackers. A guest or two leavens the family, although everyone is in the best of spirits anyway.

"Now the turkey is ready to be carved, the sage stuffing spooned to a waiting bowl and the gravy poured into a jug. The potatoes are whipped, the creamed onions given a pinch of nutmeg and the frozen garden peas a sprinkling of dried mint. Meanwhile jellies and pickles are resplendent in their china dishes, and the cut glass bowl filled with coleslaw is decorated with a sprig of holly. The mince pie is in the warming oven and the Christmas plum pudding awaits the moment when it will be carried to the dining room table alight with brandy.

"Christmas Day and Christmas week provide an opportunity to slow down, to read a new book, to gather with the family over a jigsaw puzzle and to visit with neighbours.

"Weather permitting, it is a time for sleighing, tobogganing, skiing and skating parties. Sometimes there is a big bonfire in the pasture, with mulled wine and hot dogs, followed by coffee, mince tarts and Christmas cake back at the ranch house."

★ THE HISTORIC O'KEEFE RANCH ★

CORNELIUS AND MARY ANN O'Keefe loved to entertain graciously and lavishly every Christmas Day in their elegant home near Vernon in the North Okanagan Valley of British Columbia. Sleigh bells jingled as people from Vernon and the surrounding countryside arrived at the ranch in horse-drawn cutters to attend the open house. Champagne toasts started off the merriment. Then guests visited and helped themselves at a table laden with such specialties such as cold tongue in mould, spiced beef, tomato aspic, fruitcake, ginger cake, shortbread, and ginger cookies. These had all been prepared by the family cook, Louis Wong, under the watchful eye of Mrs. O'Keefe.

The ranch was a centre of social activity and remained in the family for ninety-one years before becoming a historic site in the 1960s.

The family had much to be thankful for. Life had not always been easy. Mary Ann came as a bride

Mary Ann O'Keefe. THE HISTORIC O'KEEFE RANCH

to a log house heated only by two stoves, one in the kitchen and one in the parlour. Cooking, baking, eating, bathing, washing clothes, and dressing were all done in the kitchen. There was no indoor plumbing. Roads were primitive, and the ranch at first was isolated. Mary Ann was one of only a few European women in the whole Okanagan Valley.

Mary Ann bore nine children in ten years, so when her husband was able to build the lovely Queen Anne–style mansion, there was cause for celebration. She enjoyed her new home for only thirteen years before she died of a massive stroke. Later, Cornelius married Elizabeth Tierney, forty years younger than himself, and they had five more children.

From Ken Mather's Home Sweet Home: A History of the Historic O'Keefe Ranch, 1867–1977 *(1995)*

≋ TONGUE IN MOULD ≋
WITH MUSTARD SAUCE

At the turn of the century, fashionable hostesses served jellied tongue at picnics, card parties, dances, and receptions. This recipe was developed by Bessie Emms, who was born near Wainwright, Alberta, but spent most of her life in Calgary. She suggested unmoulding it for the buffet table, slicing thinly, and serving on a dark bread with a dab of mustard sauce.

Soak fresh tongue in corned-beef brine for 3 weeks before cooking or, if you prefer, purchase a pickled tongue from your butcher. Large tongues are somewhat coarser in texture than small tongues.

COOKING THE TONGUE
Rinse the tongue. Place in large pot and cover with juice, wine or beer, pickling spice, and enough water to cover. Gently simmer for 7 to 10 hours. Cool. Remove tongue from liquid and devein. Place in a bowl or mould (a large empty cottage-cheese container makes a nice container).

MOULDING THE TONGUE
Heat consommé, sherry, and dissolved gelatin. Pour over tongue. Cover with a plate and place a weight on top of the plate to press the tongue firmly into the mould. Refrigerate overnight or all day. Unmould and serve with mustard sauce. Note: This mould is most attractive made with 2 tongues.

MUSTARD SAUCE
This smooth, gentle sauce is a good accompaniment for cold tongue, cold ham, spiced beef, and corned beef.

Mix all ingredients together in a heavy saucepan. Simmer for 20 minutes. Cool. Serve with cold tongue or baked ham.

COOKING THE TONGUE

1 pickled tongue

2 cups (500 mL) fruit juice (apple, orange, or juice from tinned fruits)

½ cup (125 mL) white wine or beer

1 tbsp (15 mL) pickling spice

MOULDING THE TONGUE

½ can consommé

2 tbsp (30 mL) sherry

½ tbsp (7 mL) gelatin, dissolved in a little water

MUSTARD SAUCE

2 cups (500 mL) brown sugar

2 tbsp (30 mL) flour

½ cup (125 mL) dry mustard

½ tsp (2 mL) salt

1 cup (250 mL) vinegar

1 cup (250 mL) water

2 beef bouillon cubes

⫸ CHICKEN 'N' DUMPLINGS ⫷

4 lbs (2 kg) stewing chicken

1 medium onion, sliced

2 stalks celery and leaves

1 bay leaf

6 tbsp (100 mL) flour

½ cup (125 mL) cream

1 tsp (5 mL) salt

1 tsp (5 mL) sage

½ tsp (2 mL) thyme

⅛ tsp (½ mL) pepper

DUMPLINGS

1 ½ cups (375 mL) flour

2 tsp (10 mL) baking powder

¾ tsp (3 mL) salt

1 egg

1 cup (250 mL) milk

Serves 6

Monica Hopkins attended the Priddis Fair in 1910 and admired the jars of preserved chicken exhibited on the long trestle tables. "They made my mouth water they looked so delicious. I longed to retire to bed and be fed an invalid fare of chicken and fruit." These and other memories are recalled in her manuscript Log Cabin and We Two, 1909–10, *at the Glenbow Archives in Calgary.*

CUT CHICKEN INTO serving pieces and place in a large pot. Cover chicken with water. Add the onion, celery, and bay leaf. Cover and simmer for 3 hours or until tender.

Remove chicken. Strain and measure broth. There should be approximately 4 cups of broth. If there is more, reduce by boiling; if less, add water.

Mix flour with a little cold water to form a smooth paste. Stir into broth and heat until thickened. Add cream, salt, sage, thyme, and pepper. Remove the chicken from bones and return meat to gravy.

Prepare dumplings and drop by spoonfuls into hot gravy. Cover and simmer for 20 minutes without removing lid.

Serve chicken surrounded by dumplings on a large, deep platter.

DUMPLINGS

Sift flour, baking powder, and salt into a bowl. Mix egg and milk, and stir into the dry ingredients. Drop into hot gravy and simmer, covered, for 20 minutes.

★ RANCH WOMEN ★

RANCH WOMEN CAME from all levels of society. There were mail-order brides and titled ladies, illiterate housemaids and talented poets. They were plain-looking and beautiful, young and old. Whatever their origins and attributes, these women had to adapt to the new life and work hard in order to survive in the West.

On large ranches their work was generally confined to the house and gardens. On small ranches they participated in all aspects of ranch work. A few led privileged lives, with hired help and a governess for their children. However, in a country where there were at least two men for every woman, it wasn't long before the female help was courted and married by a lonely bachelor, and the "privileged" woman had to do her own work.

For hard work, consider Mrs. Bennett, who made and sold 108 pounds of butter each week besides attending to other chores, wrote Jock Carpenter in his book *Fifty Dollar Bride.* Or Marie Rose Smith, who tanned leather, made soap, dried meat, preserved berries, and gave birth to seventeen children, unattended by a doctor.

Mrs. Burke, a young bride from Ireland, lived on an isolated ranch in the foothills. Years later, her granddaughter, Meriel Hayden, remembers her saying that she "longed to hear my own name." Once, she was alone on the ranch with three small children during a blizzard. Fearful of a chimney fire, she dared not leave them alone. "I couldn't even milk the cow for eight days," she told Meriel.

Ranch women loved a good time too! Bea Godden rode a horse sixty miles to Calgary to go to a dance. On a fall day Mrs. Macleay liked nothing better than to hitch her horse to a buggy and drive off to hunt prairie chickens. Mrs. Boulton at Aldersyde sat in her rocker and fished with a willow rod, using grasshoppers for bait. Mrs. Billy Cochrane rode to the hounds with as much vigour as she had back home in England, even though in Canada she had to chase a coyote instead of a fox.

Women such as these have left a legacy of pride and independence as strong as that of the men with whom they shared their lives.

Mrs. Harry Denning with two prairie chickens ready for plucking. Prairie chickens, partridges, ducks, geese, and large game were all part of the ranchers' menu. Like most ranch women, Mrs. Denning was handy with a gun.
GLENBOW ARCHIVES, NA-2674-17

ROAST WILD DUCK

2 average-sized ducks, plucked,
    drawn, and washed

¼ cup (50 mL) oil

1 tsp (5 mL) salt

¼ tsp (1 mL) pepper

6 strips bacon

1 can consommé or 1 cup
    (250 mL) beef broth

¼ cup Madeira wine

_____

Serves 4

Hunting was and is still both a sport and a means of providing fresh meat for the table.

MIX THE OIL, salt, and pepper and brush over skin surface. Place birds on a rack in a roasting pan, breast side up. Cover with bacon strips. Roast at 425°F (220°C) for approximately 1 to 1½ hours (depending on whether you like duck rare, medium, or well done).

Remove from oven. Skim off most of fat in pan. Stir consommé and Madeira wine into the drippings to make a sauce. Heat.

Serve ducks on a platter with Madeira sauce in a gravy bowl. Drizzle the sauce over the ducks.

 ★ A BAKE OVEN ★

AS A BRIDE, Susan Louisa Allison rode sidesaddle over the rugged Hope Trail to become the first white woman to settle in the Similkameen Valley of British Columbia. Shortly thereafter she and her husband established a ranch called Sunnyside (now Westbank) on Okanagan Lake. She became a good neighbour to the surrounding First Nations and from them learned to cure fish and dry venison. The family lost two homes, one to fire and one to flood, and lived for a time in a tent. With her children's help, Susan built an outdoor bake oven and continued to produce delicious meals.

"It was hard work cooking without a stove. I thought that with all hands helping I could build a bake oven. This I did on the banks of a river using cobblestones and clay. All hands gathered the stones, Will and Beatrice mixed mud, Lily packed it to me and I built it. Someone found a half melted door from the old stove which made a good door for the new oven.

"One day near June I had put three ducks nicely dressed, and a huge custard into the oven, and all was cooked ready to be eaten by hungry people. I had no tea or coffee so I browned some dried peas and used them for coffee, which was also ready. Two well-dressed men rode up and said they were starving so I gave them something to eat... I dished up the dinner and told them to sit down. I thought there would be enough for us but no, they ate all the ducks and pudding. They talked French thinking I couldn't understand them. They said my bread was like cake and the ducks the best they had ever tasted. I felt proud of the oven after that."

Susan Allison in A Pioneer Gentlewoman in British Columbia, *edited by Margaret A. Ormsby.*

★ RODEOS ★

A COWBOY'S LIFE always revolved around horses and cattle. Even on Sunday, the usual day off, he was apt to wander over to the corral for a little bronco busting with the other cowhands.

This impromptu fun grew into organized rodeos with bucking-horse competitions, steer-riding events, calf-roping exhibitions, and a purse for the winners. At first there were no fenced areas and no pickup men. A horse was saddled in a narrow chute or roped and snubbed to another saddle horse in an open corral while the rider mounted. There was no time limit to the ride. It lasted from the time the horse was turned loose until the cowboy rode it to a standstill or was bucked off.

Each year the number of rodeos grew, until there are now professional rodeos in towns and villages from Manitoba to British Columbia, with more and more cowboy participants and an increasing number of fans.

Some of the more spectacular events are the bareback and saddle-bronc competitions with jumping, twisting broncs and the Brahma bull rides with crazily spinning, dangerous bulls. Calf roping, steer wrestling, wild-cow milking, steer decorating, barrel racing, and cutting-horse contests demonstrate the skill and timing of the competitors and their highly trained horses. However, for sheer action nothing compares with the creaking, dust-spewing chuckwagon races.

It is said that the chuckwagon races started during the 1892 roundup on the Walrond Range, now part of southern Alberta. Four large ranches had each sent a chuckwagon and cook along to feed its own crew of cowboys. The wagons were camped side by side, and the men, caught up in the excitement of the roundup, engaged in good-natured joshing. When the roundup boss ordered the wagons to a new location, the chuckwagon cooks threw in their equipment and raced off, each anxious to obtain the best campsite.

What a race it was! In *Leaves from the Medicine Tree* (High River Pioneers' and Old Timers' Association), describes how one of the wagons lost its stove. The door on the mess cupboard of another was jolted open, and the pots and pans and plates were scattered across the countryside.

Today, the chuckwagon races have become one of the most exciting events on the rodeo circuit.

The Big Gap Ranchers' Roundup in the Neutral Hills near the Alberta–Saskatchewan border, *circa* 1919. The event, one of the largest rodeos of the decade, was in honour of the returning World War I veterans. GLENBOW ARCHIVES, NC-6-3422

⚛ BEEF IN A PIT ⚛

Roasting beef slowly in a pit has provided a wonderful atmosphere and flavour at many special celebrations. It takes up to 14 hours to prepare the fire and then cook the beef, so this is a job to be taken seriously. The following directions were provided by Harry Smith of Nanton, Alberta. A similar method is printed in the British Columbia Women's Institute Centennial Cook Book *(Mitchell Press Ltd., 1958).*

SELECT BONED AND rolled 20-lb (10 kg) roasts, allowing 1 lb for every 2 to 3 persons. Prepare a pit in the ground that is 4 feet (1.3 m) deep, 3 feet (1 m) wide, and 8 feet (2.6 m) long. For smaller amounts of meat, the pit can be shorter in width and length, but it should be 3 feet (1 m) deep.

Make a fire in the pit using hardwood or applewood (do not use wood that contains pitch). The fire should burn for 2 to 3 hours, with fuel added as needed, until there is a 2-foot (60 cm) bed of coals. Level coals with a rake and remove any unburned pieces of wood. Place metal bars across the pit ends. Place a sheet of galvanized metal (such as for roofing) over the bars, enough to cover ⅓ of the pit on each end. Cover the metal with earth.

While the coals are being prepared, the meat should be salted and peppered and wrapped in foil or heavy brown waxed paper (available from a butcher shop). The wrapped meat is then covered with burlap and tied with heavy cord. (Do not use binder twine.) Wet the burlap-wrapped meat by dipping parcels in a pail of water. Lower the meat through the open part of the pit , laying the parcels so that there is space between them. The parcels can be moved by means of a long stick with a hook on the end.

Cover the centre with metal and more earth, about 4 inches (10 cm), to prevent steam from escaping. Avoid air holes. The burlap will not burn as long as there are no air holes. Cooking time is about 10 hours.

Lift parcels out and cut off the burlap. Carve the meat and serve on plates or open-faced buns and enjoy.

★ COWBOY MANNERS ★

MANY PEOPLE BELIEVE that cowboys were unmannered. That's not so—they had their own rules for good manners and proper deportment, and those rules were strictly observed.

At the chuckwagon, they held back until the cook yelled, "Come 'n' get it" or gave some other signal. Then they helped themselves and sat down cross-legged to eat. They did not wait for others to be served, nor did they make polite dinner conversation. "Eat now and talk later." That was the rule. Hungry men could go back for seconds, but they never took the last portion of food unless everyone else had been served first.

There were rules regarding the wearing of cowboy hats. Generally, hats remained on the head. Only when eating at a proper table in the presence of a lady was the hat removed, but even then, leaving it on was not regarded as offensive. When eating outside during a rainstorm, the hat was pushed to the back of the head so any water collected in the wide brim would run down the back instead of onto the dinner plate.

Personal privacy was respected. If a stranger rode into cow camp, he was invited to pull off his saddle and "come 'n' eat." Neither the stranger's name nor place of origin was asked. Such information was considered private. Only if the stranger was given a job did the foreman inquire, "What are we to call you?"

To address a fellow cowboy by his last name would be an extreme insult. The last name was seldom used, sometimes not even known. A man could go for a long time being known simply as Hank or Pete. He was judged on his loyalty to the ranch and his ability as a rider.

Cowboys held women in great esteem. Perhaps they felt that all women who dared to brave the hardships of the West were worthy of admiration. Whatever the reason, women could travel anywhere in complete safety, with respectful assistance given at every turn.

Rancher Bert Sheppard, in his book *Spitzee Days* (John D. McAra, 1971), recalled the gallantry exhibited by a western cowboy in the town of High River, Alberta. In those days the train used to make a forty-five-minute shunting stop. During this time the passengers disembarked for a cup of coffee and snack at Mrs. Robertson's station

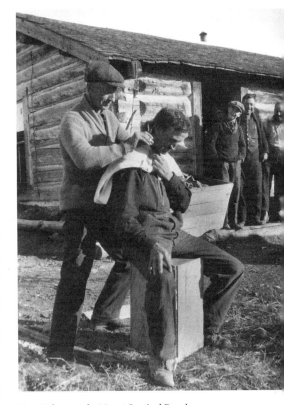

Tony Nelson, at the Mount Sentinel Ranch near Nanton, having his hair trimmed in preparation for a dance. GLENBOW ARCHIVES, NA-2467-31

Prairie grass and bedrolls make a dinner seat for the cowboys on a roundup. Note the chuckwagon backed up so that the meal can be prepared and served from a shelter.

GLENBOW ARCHIVES, NC-39-246A

restaurant. One day a dignified lady traveller was so slow to enter and be served that she had just received her cup of steaming coffee when the train whistle sounded, warning of the departure in five minutes. The cowboy sitting at the counter sized up her predicament, reached over, and offered her his cup, saying, "Here, lady, take mine; it's been saucered and blowed."

VEGETABLES
★ AND ★
LEGUMES

☀ CUCUMBERS WITH CREAM ☀

3 cucumbers, peeled and thinly
    sliced
1 tbsp (15 mL) salt
1 small onion, finely chopped, or
    3 green onions
1 cup (250 mL) thick cream, sour
    or sweet
1 tbsp (15 mL) vinegar
2 tbsp (30 mL) sugar
freshly ground pepper to taste

_____

Serves 8 to 10

PLACE CUCUMBERS IN a bowl and sprinkle with salt. Set a weight on top of the cucumbers. Refrigerate for several hours, then pour off the juice. Mix onion(s), cream, vinegar, sugar, and pepper. Pour over the cucumbers.

☀ SCALLOPED CORN CASSEROLE ☀

2 14-oz (398 mL) cans creamed corn
2 beaten eggs
¾ cup (175 mL) milk
1 tsp (5 mL) salt
¼ tsp (1 mL) freshly ground black
    pepper
¾ cup (175 mL) soda cracker crumbs
3 tbsp (45 mL) butter, melted

_____

Serves 6

This winter vegetable dish can be served with beef, ham, pork chops, sausages, or meat loaf.

MIX CORN, EGGS, milk, salt, and pepper in a casserole. Mix half the crackers with the corn mixture. Mix the other half with the butter, and sprinkle on top of corn mixture. Bake in a 325°F (160°C) oven for about 1 hour.

Ranch house west of Fort Macleod, Alberta, *circa* 1888. GLENBOW ARCHIVES, NA-2033-1

★ SIT UP FOR A MEAL ★

BERT SHEPPARD TOLD E.G. Luxton the following story in 1958 (Glenbow Archives).

When Bea Godden returned from England, she was met in Calgary by her fiancé, Henry Sheppard. They were married that day and started at once for their home on the Paleface Ranch, some distance away.

They travelled as far as Pine Creek Stopping Place the first night and arrived at the High River Horse Ranch about suppertime the next day. Manager Phil Weinard invited them to have supper and stay the night. In their honour, he set the table with a fine white tablecloth, silverware and beautiful cut glass—all brought from England by the previous owner. By this time the new bride was quite impressed with ranch life and sat at the table with expectations of a splendid supper. At last the first and only course was brought in—a big black iron pot full of cornmeal mush.

It was the custom of the country to invite guests "to sit up for a meal," and there was no embarrassment or apology if there was a meagre supply of food on hand.

≋ SCALLOPED TOMATOES ≋

1 cup (250 mL) bread, cubed

2 tbsp (30 mL) butter

2 tbsp (30 mL) onion, chopped

14-oz (398 mL) can tomatoes

3 tbsp (45 mL) brown sugar

½ tsp (2 mL) salt

½ tsp (2 mL) dried basil

_____

Serves 3 to 4

Canned tomatoes were useful on chuckwagons and in ranch kitchens. They added flavour and colour to a rather bland diet and were frequently the only available vegetable. Cowboy Bud Cotton told me that on dry trails, cowboys drank the tomato liquid to relieve their parched throats, and when the cans were empty, they served as useful containers.

PLACE THE CUBED bread in a casserole. Melt the butter in a saucepan and lightly sauté the onions. Pour over the bread cubes. Mix the tomatoes, sugar, salt, and basil, and pour over the bread. Cover tightly with a lid or foil and bake for approximately 30 minutes in a 350°F (180°C) oven. Serve with meat loaf, ranch steak, or pork sausages.

The Lachlan McKinnon children on the LK Ranch, Dalemead, *circa* 1910. Building the LK into a beautiful and prosperous Alberta ranch was a family enterprise. GLENBOW ARCHIVES, NA-3850-1

★ THE RANCH HOME ★

"**THERE WAS WORK** for every season," Annie McKinnon Fuller told me in an interview in 1979. "Summer was spent breaking horses, rounding up cattle, branding, calving, seeding, haying, fencing, butchering. During winter, special care was given to the livestock, supplying feed, keeping a water hole open, fending off coyotes and wolves, and mending harnesses. It was quite a job to organize and keep a ranch household running smoothly. Everyone helped. When children weren't studying, they worked on the ranch: chopping wood, haying, fencing, cooking, washing dishes, cleaning house, and churning butter.

"The ranch house was home, school, and social centre to fifteen people, counting nine members of the family, the hired help, and a school governess who lived and held school in the big room upstairs.

"There were always extra people dropping in for a meal. Planks were added to the end of the dining room table until it became so long it extended right into the kitchen. Meals were informal, the food hearty and healthy. Nothing was wasted. A bone was turned into soup, with even the beef marrow eaten. Extra milk made cheese; doughnuts were made with extra lard; dried bread was the basis for bread pudding.

"We drove to town two or three times a year and loaded up on supplies: one hundred lbs of honey; cases of dried fruit; five barrels of apples every fall; one-hundred-lb bags of sugar and flour, each in five-bag lots.

"Most of the food came from the ranch itself. A cow and a pig were butchered and the meat put up for later use as corned beef, canned beef, hams, bacon, and sausages. Chickens were raised for eggs and for Sunday dinner. The vegetable garden provided fresh greens all summer and enough potatoes, turnips and carrots to store in the root house for winter use.

"Wild berries—saskatoons, chokecherries and gooseberries—were made into jam and preserves. Milk was separated, the cream used for butter and baking, the milk for drinking and puddings.

"There was fun as well as work. We had taffy pulls and hymn singing on Sunday nights. There were summer picnics and parties to which everyone went—children, parents, and the hired help."

⚜ DILLED CARROTS ⚜

8 garlic cloves

16 sprigs of dill

8 lbs (4 kg) straight 3-inch (8 cm)
    baby carrots

8 cups (2 L) white vinegar

8 cups (2 L) water

1 cup (250 mL) pickling salt

1 tsp (5 mL) white pepper

1 tsp (5 mL) mustard seed

When the Fenton Ranch holds its production sale in November, up to three hundred people turn out to inspect the cattle and ranch operations, Judy Rutledge Fenton told me in a 1981 interview in Irma, Alberta. As most of the people have travelled a great distance, it is customary to provide a roast-beef dinner at noon and a snack later in the afternoon before the guests leave for home. Six 18-pound roasts of beef, which have been in the oven since 4:00 AM, are carved and served with baked potatoes, a variety of salads, dill pickles, dilled carrots, and bread. Sixty pies or thirty jelly rolls or twenty cakes are sliced for dessert. Gallons of coffee and juice are available for drinking.

PUT A SMALL piece of garlic and a piece of dill in the bottom of each of 8 hot, sterilized quart (litre) jars. Place clean, whole carrots in each jar. Place another piece of dill on top.

Bring to a boil the vinegar, water, salt, pepper, and mustard seed. Pour over the carrots to within ½ inch (1 cm) of the top. Tighten lid. Keep in a cool storage area.

Luella Goddard on the Bow River Horse Ranch near Cochrane, Alberta, *circa* early 1900s. Women usually made their own clothes and were skilled in the art of needlework. GLENBOW ARCHIVES, NA-2084-30

⪢ CREAMED ONIONS ⪡

This vegetable dish is a good accompaniment for ranch-style steak.

PEEL ONIONS AND place in a pot with a large amount of boiling, salted water. Boil uncovered for 20 to 30 minutes, until onions are tender but still retaining their form. Drain and transfer onions to a buttered casserole dish.

To prepare cream sauce, melt butter and stir in flour. When blended, add milk slowly while stirring. Cook on low heat until thick. Add salt, pepper, and nutmeg. Pour sauce over onions.

Mix cracker crumbs and melted butter, and spread topping over onions. Sprinkle parmesan cheese over the mixture.

Bake at 350°F (180°C) for 12 to 15 minutes or until onions and sauce are hot and the crumbs lightly browned. Plan for 1 to 2 onions per person.

8 medium onions
3 tbsp (45 mL) butter
3 tbsp (45 mL) flour
2 cups (500 mL) milk
½ tsp (2 mL) salt
pinch pepper
¼ tsp (1 mL) nutmeg
½ cup (125 mL) cracker crumbs
2 tbsp (30 mL) melted butter
parmesan cheese

MARINATED ONIONS IN SOUR CREAM

2 large onions, finely sliced
½ cup (125 mL) vinegar
½ cup (125 mL) water
¾ cup (175 mL) sugar
1 cup (250 mL) sour cream
salt and pepper to taste

Serves 10

Serve marinated onions in a bowl for guests to spoon onto open-faced hot beef sandwiches or beef on a bun.

COVER THE ONIONS with vinegar, water, and sugar to marinate. Refrigerate for at least 6 hours. Drain well. Mix with sour cream, salt, and pepper.

PICKLED BEETS

6 lbs (3 kg) beets
4 cups (1 L) vinegar
2 cups (500 mL) water
3 cups (750 mL) sugar
1 tbsp (15 mL) mixed pickling
    spices

*Makes approximately
8 pint (0.5 L) jars*

This was a popular pickle, probably because beets are easy to grow. Small young beets are best, but large beets can be used successfully too.

COOK BEETS IN boiling water until tender (this may take up to 2 hours). Peel. If beets are large, cut them into thick slices; if small, leave whole. Combine vinegar, sugar, and spices. Bring to a boil and simmer for 10 minutes. Pack beets into sterilized jars and cover with hot liquid. Seal and store in a cool place.

⚛ TURNIP PUFF ⚛

In Leaves from the Medicine Tree, *High River pioneers recalled a popular stopping place. As there were no hotels and restaurants, bullwhackers and cowboys liked to stay at Joe Trollinger's Stopping House on Mosquito Creek, halfway between Fort Macleod and Calgary. Joe's wife, Lucy, grew a vegetable garden, which was unusual for those times. Her menus included generous piles of turnips and provided a welcome change to the early rangeland diet of sowbelly and beans.*

Turnips continued to be a staple food on winter menus, as they were one of the few vegetables that kept well in the basements and root cellars of the early ranch homes. This recipe is rather special and could be served for Thanksgiving and Christmas dinner.

4 cups (1 L) boiled, mashed turnips
4 tbsp (60 mL) butter
2 tsp (10 mL) sugar
1 tsp (5 mL) salt
pinch of nutmeg
pepper to taste
2 eggs, separated

ADD THE BUTTER, sugar, salt, nutmeg, pepper, and egg yolks to the turnips. Beat together. Whip the egg whites until stiff, as for meringue, and fold into the turnip mixture. Pile into a buttered 1½-quart (1.5 L) casserole dish and bake at 300° to 350°F (150° to 180°C) for 15 to 20 minutes.

MANY SOCIAL OCCASIONS for ranch people revolve around work, such as roundups and brandings.

Brands and brandings are important in the life of the ranching community. Each ranch has its own registered brand, specific in its shape and location on the animal. The brand denotes ownership, controls cattle rustling, and prevents disputes with neighbouring ranches.

June is the usual time for branding spring calves, before the animals are herded out to summer pasture. At the same time, any older stock newly acquired by the ranch are branded as well.

Ranches hold their own brandings or work with several other outfits, taking turns moving from one place to another. With help, they can brand as many as three or four hundred calves in one day.

As many as one hundred people might come to a branding, most of them to help in some way. The hosts are up early to wrangle, saddle, and bridle the horses. Work begins early, with skilled riders and their cutting horses roping calves and hauling them bawling and protesting to the corrals, where they are castrated, earmarked, inoculated, and branded. Most of the people work. Those not working sit on the corral rails and enjoy the bustle of animals, people, fires, and the outdoors.

The women on the ranch have been preparing for this event well ahead of time. Neighbours help by bringing enormous pans of cakes, cookies, and pies. Nobody comes empty-handed to a branding.

The noon meal is brought out and served buffet style from the back of a truck bed, although a few ranchers still like to keep with tradition and bring out their chuckwagon on these special occasions. Food is simple: pots of beans, a hearty stew, salads, homemade buns, choice of pie, and coffee.

A branding scene at Bar U Ranch, *circa* 1919. Note the fire, the branding irons, and the wrestlers holding the animals down. Local First Nations people worked as wrestlers for the day and helped with many other operations on the ranch.
GLENBOW ARCHIVES, NB-16-260

Work continues until all the calves have been branded and the cows dehorned. Cows and calves are turned out on the range and the branding is finished for another year.

Now the visiting and celebrating begins. Prime rib roasts or a hip of beef have been barbecued. An assortment of salads, homemade buns, and pies—apple, rhubarb, raisin, saskatoon—are spread out on a long table. Talk turns to cattle and horses and brandings of long ago.

Baked beans are a tradition at brandings and other western celebrations. This baked-bean dish is hearty enough to be served as a main course.

BROWN THE BEEF. Sauté the onions. Add to beans. Combine remaining ingredients and add to bean mixture. Bake slowly in a 300°F (150°C) oven for 1 to 2 hours. Time will depend on the type of baking dish used. A heavy bean pot will take up to 2 hours.

2 lbs (1 kg) ground beef

2 medium onions, chopped

2 28-fl.-oz (796 mL) cans beans

⅔ cup (150 mL) brown sugar

⅓ cup (75 mL) vinegar

1 cup (250 mL) ketchup or canned tomatoes

2 tsp (10 mL) dry mustard

2 tsp (10 mL) Worcestershire sauce

Serves 8

★ THE BEAUTY OF BEANS ★

BULLWHACKERS, COWBOYS, RANCHERS, and Royal Canadian Mounted Police officers sat down to many meals of baked beans. Dry navy beans were easy to store and kept well. They could be cooked in a heavy Dutch oven over the coals of a campfire or in the oven of a kitchen range. When cooked, they remained fresh for several days. A foreman in the Cariboo known for his toughness was heard to say, "Put a few navy beans in your pocket, and you can stay out on the job for a week."

Dorothy Allen-Gray, whose husband was with the RCMP for thirty years, recalls this story being told at a gathering of retired officers: One Mountie serving at a northern outpost kept himself in quick frozen dinners all winter. He baked an enormous pot of beans and then spooned them into long ladies' stockings. These he hung on nails outside his shack, where they soon froze. When hungry, he took his axe, chopped off the required portion of frozen beans, and heated them for a quick dinner.

☰ BULLWHACKERS' ☰
BAKED BEANS

←————————→

2½ cups (625 mL/450 g) navy beans

½ cup (125 mL) brown sugar

½ cup (125 mL) fancy molasses

¼ cup (50 mL) cold black coffee or

    ¼ tsp (1 mL) instant coffee

¼ cup (50 mL) canned tomatoes

2 tsp (10 mL) dry mustard

2 tsp (10 mL) salt

½ lb (250 g) salt pork or side

    bacon, cubed

————

Serves 6

WASH THE BEANS. Place in a large pot, cover with water, and leave to soak overnight. The next day, add enough water to cover the beans and boil until just tender (¾ to 1 hour). If you have forgotten to soak the beans overnight, simmer them for approximately 2 hours or until soft. Drain.

Place the beans in a bean pot or casserole. Add remaining ingredients and enough water to cover the beans. Bake uncovered at 300°F (150°c) for 5 to 6 hours. Check occasionally during cooking and add more water if necessary, enough to keep the top beans from drying out.

 ★ BULL TRAINS ★

THE CANADIAN WEST has been the setting of many colourful scenes in its short history: First Nations gathered in ceremonial robes, Red River carts, scarlet-coated North West Mounted Policemen, stagecoaches, and majestic cattle drives. A unique sight was the bull trains, hauling groceries, dry goods, building supplies, and even a little whisky from Fort Benton, Montana, to the new settlements of Fort Walsh, Fort Macleod, High River, and Calgary.

Bull trains consisted of five or six strings of plodding oxen and wagons that could stretch across the country for half a mile, dust drifting up in little clouds as they moved along. Each string consisted of eight or ten pairs of oxen pulling three freight wagons coupled together like railroad cars.

John D. Higinbotham, in *When the West Was Young* (Ryerson Press, 1933; The Herald Printers,

1978), explained that the drivers were called bullwhackers because they rode up and down the line, snapping their eighteen-strand snake whips, swearing, and shouting, "Gee up, you long-horned, slab-sided prairie perambulatory sons of perdition! Gee up or I'll knock every hair off your measly hide!"

The bull trains covered ten miles a day and took a week to travel from Calgary to Fort Macleod. At night the oxen grazed while the men gathered buffalo chips for their cooking fires. Grub was simple—beans in a Dutch oven, buried in the embers of the fire and left to slow-cook overnight; a little sowbelly (bullwhackers and cowboys frequently referred to salt pork as "sowbelly" or "rattlesnake pork"), sliced and fried; fresh bannock, with enough baked to last the next day too; and strong black coffee.

BREADS
★ AND ★
QUICK BREADS

 AIR BUNS

½ cup (125 mL) warm water

1 tsp (5 mL) sugar

1 tbsp (15 mL) yeast (1 package)

3½ cups (875 mL) warm water

½ cup (125 mL) sugar

½ cup (125 mL) vegetable oil

2 tsp (10 mL) salt

1 tbsp (15 mL) vanilla

8 to 10 cups (2 to 2.5 L) flour

_____

Makes 48 buns

Bread making used to require the preparation of a flour-yeast sponge the night before baking. If kept warm all night, this sponge would be nicely risen by morning—no small task in houses with wood-burning stoves and fires that died out. Ranch wife Monica Hopkins wrote in Log Cabin and We Two*: "These evenings I wrap my bread in a blanket and Billie's fur coat, put it in one of the wicker chairs and cover [it] all up with a travelling rug and you should see it next morning, right up to the very top of the bread pan."*

With today's fast-rising yeast, you can be finished making bread within three hours of starting. This recipe produces feather-light buns that can be served anytime, at picnics, brandings, and barbecues.

POUR ½ CUP (125 mL) of water into a large mixing bowl. Dissolve the teaspoon of sugar, sprinkle yeast on top, and leave for 10 minutes. Combine remaining water and sugar, vegetable oil, salt, and vanilla and add to the yeast mixture. Beat in as much of the flour as possible; knead in the remainder. Knead well for 8 to 10 minutes.

Cover with a tea towel and leave in a warm place to rise for 1 hour. Shape the dough into round buns and place on a cookie sheet, about 20 to a 12 × 18 inch (30 × 45 cm) sheet. Cover again with a tea towel and let rise for approximately 1½ hours. Bake at 400°F (200°C) for 12 to 15 minutes.

Mrs. Fred Ings feeding poultry at the Midway Ranch, Nanton, Alberta, *circa* 1911.
GLENBOW ARCHIVES, NA-2368-6

★ THE FIRST BATCH ★

THIS PIECE BY Erica Woodward appeared in *The Golden Curtain Rises*, created by the Co-operative Women's Guild of Swift Current, Saskatchewan, in 1964. It is reproduced here by permission of her family:

"We had just moved to our place near Swift Current and mother had never tried making bread before. There she was in the kitchen, banging the cupboard doors, slamming the oven of the new Kitchen Queen, tears of frustration in her eyes, angry words on her lips. Dad heard the commotion and came in. He took one look at those hard, brown blocks spread out on the kitchen table and then went over and put his arms around her.

"Next morning he woke us children and motioned us to follow him to the creek bank where he had only yesterday cut steps in the moist clay. He stopped at the first step, fished one of the dry loaves out of his bag, set it firmly on the clay step, marked its size, lifted it, cut a neat hole, then fitted the loaf perfectly into the hole to form a step. Then he embedded the second loaf in the second step and right down the line until the six loaves graced the six steps as if they had been made for that purpose. Then we fetched mother to share in the admiration of our new concrete-like steps leading to the creek. Well, we all laughed so hard we hardly had strength to make it back to the house.

"But mother was not beaten. She tackled bread baking again and again and soon was able to turn out six beautiful, golden crusted loaves. Dad while munching a sample with obvious satisfaction said it was just as well since there were no more steps to make."

≡ CINNAMON ROLLS ≡

PREPARING THE PAN

¼ cup (50 mL) butter or margarine

sprinkling of brown sugar

2 tsp (10 mL) cinnamon

1 tbsp (15 mL) water

PREPARING THE ROLLS

½ batch of air buns dough (see
     page 50)

3 tbsp (45 mL) softened butter
     or margarine

½ cup (125 mL) white sugar

4 tsp (20 mL) cinnamon

PREPARING THE PAN

Melt butter or margarine in a 9 × 13-inch (23 × 33 cm) cake pan. Add a sprinkling of brown sugar, enough to make a thin layer of the butter-sugar mixture. Sprinkle with cinnamon and water.

PREPARING THE ROLLS

Roll the bread dough into an oblong about 9 × 18 inches (23 × 46 cm). Spread with softened butter or margarine. Sprinkle with white sugar and cinnamon. Beginning at the longest side, roll up the dough and pinch the edges together. Cut the roll into 1-inch (2.5 cm) slices and place the slices a little distance apart in the prepared cake pan. Cover with a tea towel and let rise until double in bulk, 35 to 40 minutes.

Bake at 375°F (190°C) for 25 to 30 minutes (less if you use a Pyrex pan). Remove the rolls from the oven immediately and invert the pan.

The cook adds flour and water to his sourdough mixture while the nighthawk looks on. It was the nighthawk's job to tend the horses through the night, from 8:00 PM until after breakfast. He had a few other duties around camp, but mostly he slept or watched the cook during the day. GLENBOW ARCHIVES, NB-H-16-455

≋ SOURDOUGH STARTER ≋

IN A LARGE BOWL or jar (plastic, glass, or ceramic) that will hold at least 4 cups (1 L) of sourdough, dissolve the yeast in lukewarm water. Stir in the flour and sugar, and beat the mixture until smooth. Cover with cheesecloth or plastic wrap and let stand at room temperature until bubbly, at least 3 days before using. Stir 2 or 3 times a day. If the room is warm and you wish to slow fermentation, place mixture in the refrigerator for a few hours. When the starter is ready to use, it will give off a delicious, sour, yeasty odour. The flavour improves as it is used. If the starter turns orange or smells like vinegar, discard it and start again. This can occur if fermentation is too rapid or if there is not enough nutrient to feed upon.

1 tsp (5 mL) yeast
2 cups (500 mL) lukewarm water
2 cups (500 mL) all-purpose flour
1 tsp (5 mL) sugar

TO KEEP THE STARTER GOING

Every time you remove a portion of sourdough, replenish the stock by adding equal amounts of flour and water to bring it back to the original amount. Let it stand for one day before using. Stir the mixture each day. If you are not using the starter every 2 or 3 days, store it in the refrigerator to slow fermentation. Bring it back to room temperature before using. If refrigerated and not used within 10 days, feed the starter with flour and water or 1 teaspoon (5 mL) sugar, or freeze it. If the starter is frozen, thaw and reactivate with a little warm water.

✺ SOURDOUGH BREAD ✺

1 tbsp (15 mL) dry yeast

1½ cups (375 mL) lukewarm water

1 cup (250 mL) sourdough

2 tbsp (30 mL) sugar

2 tsp (10 mL) salt

4½ cups (1 L) flour

½ tsp (2 mL) baking soda

IN A LARGE BOWL, dissolve yeast in lukewarm water. Stir in sourdough, sugar, and salt. Stir in 4 cups of the flour, a cup at a time. The dough will be sticky. Cover with a cloth and leave in a warm place until doubled in bulk, approximately 1½ hours.

When the dough has risen, mix in remaining ½ cup of flour and baking soda. Turn onto a floured board and knead until dough is satiny and soft. Divide into 4 pieces and shape into loaves. Place on greased baking sheet. Make three slashes about ¼ inch (1 cm) deep in top of each loaf. Leave in a warm, draft-free spot until doubled in bulk, about 40 minutes. Bake at 375°F (190°C) oven for approximately 30 minutes or until lightly browned.

 ★ SOURDOUGH ON THE WAGON ★

"MULLIGAN JACK," AS he was known to cowboys on the Circle Bar Ranch, became famous for his cooking. He fried up generous steaks, made his own bread, and was up at dawn to have sourdough pancakes ready to feed the hungry cowboys before they rode out.

When he packed the chuckwagon with supplies, he always brought along a keg of sourdough starter. He carefully tended it, fed it regularly, and kept it warm, sometimes wrapping it in a blanket and taking it to bed with him.

He wasn't always a chuckwagon cook. He was born Jack Thomas in Detroit, Michigan, and went to Montana at the age of seventeen to be a cowboy. He came to Canada with the I.G. Baker outfit and later worked for Pat Burns. It was only after he broke both arms in an accident that he turned his talents to chuckwagon cooking. There, he left his legacy.

From Eva Delday's Brooks: Between the Red Deer and the Bow *(D.W. Friesen & Sons Ltd., 1975)*

❧ BACHELOR'S BANNOCK ❧

Bannock was the bread eaten by fur traders, early settlers, freighters, First Nations, and cowboys. Cooks varied proportions and ingredients according to their own liking and the ingredients on hand. They used flour, salt, soda (baking powder was scarce and not very reliable), a little water or milk, and melted fat—bacon fat, salt-pork fat, or beef drippings. It was usually made round, about 10 inches in diameter and 2 to 3 inches thick, with an evenly browned crust and a fairly light, soft texture. When several loaves had to be cooked on a campfire, they were left in the frying pan until well crusted, then propped up against stones, facing the fire, to continue baking. Although best when fresh and warm, bannock was frequently made ahead of time for long pack trips and stored in a "grub box."

2 cups (500 mL) flour
2 tbsp (30 mL) baking powder
1 tsp (5 mL) salt
⅓ cup (75 mL) lard or butter
1¾ cups (450 mL) water
lard for frying

MIX THE FLOUR, baking powder, salt, fat, and water. Melt a chunk of lard in a large frying pan or Dutch oven. Spread the bannock in the pan. Cook on one side until well browned and crusted, then turn it over and do the other side. If the pan is not large enough to cook all of the batter at once, divide into two or three portions and cook each portion separately.

A cowboy washing his clothes. GLENBOW ARCHIVES, NC-43-10

 ★ CARIBOO BACHELOR ★

DURING PIONEER RANCHING days, the Cariboo region was an isolated, lonely area. A bachelor could go for weeks without hearing or seeing another human. Sometimes he became so accustomed to the isolation that any social contact was avoided.

Such was the case of Charlie Jones in the Meadow Lake area [in northwestern Saskatchewan]. He was over sixty and had lived alone for a long time. In his book *Cariboo Cowboy*, Harry Marriott recalled finding his way to Charlie's cabin one bitterly cold day. As he was a long distance from any suitable place to camp, he climbed down from his horse and asked permission to spend the night.

After putting his horse in the barn and feeding it a bit of hay, he went inside and stood close to the cookstove to warm up. Charlie was mixing a pan of biscuits for supper. Harry hadn't been standing there for more than a minute when Charlie barked, "Harry, I'm going to make you a fire in the other cabin and you can sit there. I'll call you when I'm ready fer yer to eat."

Harry asked Charlie not to go to all that trouble and offered to sit up all night near the stove, but Charlie shook his head. "God almighty, I just can't cook nor nothin' if someone is in the same room." He walked out and made a fire in the other cabin. Harry followed and sat there until he was called back for supper. During the meal there was not a word spoken. Afterwards, Harry got up, went to the other cabin, and sat there until it was time to crawl under some blankets and go to sleep.

Later Charlie explained, "You know, I just don't want nobody to talk to me, Harry. If anyone talks to me it just gets me right off my chain of thought, and I don't like it worth a darn."

Cowboy Bud Cotton described making biscuits when trailing cattle. "You open the flour sack and make a little hollow in the flour, add a little soda and bacon grease, and add a cup of water from the creek. Mix it all up, form your biscuits, and you cook them in the frying pan over a nice fire." He recalled that the trail name for biscuits was "belly busters."

"Belly busters," "dough gods," "hot rocks," "sinkers"—cowboys had their own meaningful names for biscuits, which were served with bacon drippings or butter and dipped in corn syrup or molasses.

2 cups (500 mL) flour

4 tsp (20 mL) baking powder

1 tsp (5 mL) cream of tartar

½ tsp (2 mL) salt

2 tsp (10 mL) sugar

½ cup (125 mL) fat (butter or shortening)

¾ cup (175 mL) milk

Makes 16 to 20 biscuits

SIFT THE FLOUR, baking powder, cream of tartar, salt, and sugar together into a mixing bowl. Work the fat into the flour with your fingers until the mixture resembles coarse meal. Make a hollow in the centre, pour in the milk, and stir. The mixture should hold together but not be too dry. Gently knead the dough a few times.

Pat or roll out on a lightly floured board to a thickness of ⅔ inch (1.5 cm). Cut with a round cutter (or the edge of an empty tin can). Bake at 475°F (240°C) for 10 to 15 minutes or until lightly browned.

☀ CORN BREAD ☀

1½ cups (375 mL) cornmeal

2½ cups (625 mL) milk

2 eggs, beaten

½ cup (125 mL) melted fat or
   cooking oil

2 cups (500 mL) flour

¾ cup (175 mL) sugar

2 tbsp (30 mL) baking powder

1 tsp (5 mL) salt

Corn bread, or johnnycake, was baked in cake tins, cast-iron frying pans, or muffin tins. It was served hot with butter and jam for breakfast, as an accompaniment to a main course, or with syrup for dessert.

COMBINE CORNMEAL, milk, eggs, and fat. Let stand for 10 minutes. Sift flour, sugar, baking powder, and salt together. Stir into cornmeal mixture. Grease a 9 × 13-inch (23 × 33 cm) cake can or a large cast-iron frying pan. Pour in batter. Bake at 400°F (200°C) for approximately 30 minutes. Alternatively, bake in greased muffin pans for about 15 to 20 minutes.

☀ CHARLIE'S DOUGHNUTS ☀

3 eggs

¾ cup (175 mL) sugar

3 tbsp (45 mL) melted butter

3 cups (750 mL) all-purpose flour

5 tsp (25 mL) baking powder

½ tsp (2 mL) cinnamon

½ tsp (2 mL) nutmeg

¾ cup (175 mL) buttermilk

fat for frying

The recipe that belonged to Charlie Lehr, an old-time chuckwagon cook, is in Charlie's notebook at the High River Museum in High River, Alberta: "Two teacups sugar, 3 eggs, 1½ tea cups buttermilk, 2 teaspoons saleratus [baking soda], 1 teaspoon salt, 6 tablespoons melted lard, flour enough to roll nicely. Boil or fry in lard."

This recipe, revised for today, makes doughnuts that taste just as good as they did in Charlie's time.

BEAT THE EGGS and sugar together. Add the butter. Sift the dry ingredients and stir into the egg mixture alternately with the buttermilk. The dough will be very soft. Chill for approximately 1 hour. Roll out on a generously floured board. Cut with a doughnut cutter. Fry in 1 inch of hot fat (350°F/180°C), turning once, until light golden brown. Remove from fat and sprinkle with sugar.

★ THE RANCH COOK ★

MANY OF THE big ranches had a separate cookhouse where the cowboys ate. Here the cook worked and lived, becoming crankier as the years went by. "Tetchy as a cook," they used to say. No wonder. He worked long hours during the day: cooking the meals, tending the chickens, milking the cows. Breakfast was early and supper was late. After washing and putting away the dishes, he took out a five-gallon lard pail and mixed up a batch of sourdough pancakes for breakfast. This last task completed, he retired to his room next to the kitchen for a short night's sleep.

Before daybreak he shuffled back to the kitchen, struck a match to the coal oil lamp, and built a fire in the wood stove. The porridge was started. The enamel coffee pot was filled with water and put on the hot part of the stove to boil. The table was set with plates, knives, forks, spoons, and cups. The long-handled cast-iron frying pan was placed on the stove to heat. Then he brought out the pail of sourdough batter that had been rising all night and stirred in a pinch of sugar. Batter was spooned into the frying pan in large dollops that spread as they cooked. When little bubbles appeared on top, meaning that the bottom side was nicely browned, he flipped the pan in such a way that the pancakes turned over in the air and came down bottom side up.

When the porridge was nicely cooked, the coffee steaming on the back of the stove, and a stack of pancakes piled in the warming oven, he opened the door, stepped out onto the porch, and rang an old cowbell.

The cowboys ate their way through the porridge, then poured a little "Charlie Taylor"—a mixture of molasses and bacon grease that was also used on biscuits—over the pancakes and washed them down with steaming coffee. Some mornings the cook fried thin beefsteaks or strips of salted pork and, if the hens were laying, eggs.

"Mow" was a cook at CC Ranch near Mosquito Creek. Many cooks on the big ranches were Chinese men who had worked during the building of the railroad and stayed on after it was completed. They opened restaurants and laundries in the small towns and played an important part in building the West. GLENBOW ARCHIVES, NA-2307-50

⚛ FLAPJACKS ⚛

2 eggs

2 cups (500 mL) liquid*

2 tbsp (30 mL) sugar

2 tbsp (30 mL) melted bacon
    fat or oil

2 cups (500 mL) all-purpose flour**

1 tbsp (15 mL) baking powder

½ tsp (2 mL) salt

VARIATIONS

*Use half milk and half water,
    or all milk.

** Use 1¼ cups (300 mL)
    all-purpose flour with
    ¾ cup (175 mL) whole-
    wheat flour or cornmeal.

CAMP SYRUP

2 cups (500 mL) brown sugar

1 cup (250 mL) water

½ tsp (2 mL) maple flavouring

Serves 4 to 6

Cowboys and chuckwagon cooks never followed a written recipe for flapjacks. They remembered the proportion of 1 to 1 for each ingredient— that is, 1 cup flour, 1 cup liquid, 1 egg, 1 rounded teaspoon of baking powder, 1 spoonful of melted fat or drippings, and a pinch of salt.

BEAT EGGS, LIQUID, sugar, and fat until blended. Sift together the remaining dry ingredients. Add to the egg mixture and beat well. Grease a frying pan lightly and drop spoonfuls of batter into the hot pan. When cakes bubble, turn and cook the other side.

CAMP SYRUP

This easy-to-prepare, delicious syrup is a good substitute for maple syrup.

Bring the brown sugar and water to a boil and simmer for approximately 5 minutes. Add the flavouring. Store in a jar in the refrigerator and serve hot or cold.

CAKES
★ AND ★
COOKIES

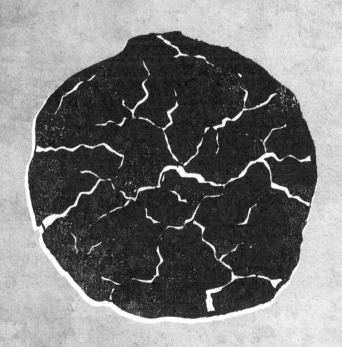

A home orchestra near Maple Creek, Saskatchewan, in 1913. Ranching families made their own fun. The walls made from squared logs have been given a light coat of calcamine. GLENBOW ARCHIVES, NA-1095-8

★ DANCING ★

BEFORE THE TURN of the century, the North West Mounted Police posts were the centre of social life, and their dances were great events on the social calendar. Thirteen police balls were held in 1880 at Fort Walsh. The three Caucasian women living there at the time—Mrs. Macleod, Mrs. Winder, and Mrs. Shurtliff—attended, as well as many of the local mixed-race ladies.

Mothers always took their babies to the dances and left them on a nearby bed, where they slept undisturbed. The exception was an occasion, recalled by Mrs. Kate de Veber in an interview by Edna Kells (Glenbow Archives, *circa* 1935), on which a couple of the cowboys thought that it would be great fun to switch baby clothes, bonnets, and blankets. When the dancing was over, the mothers sleepily picked up their babies and went home. The next morning when they each saw a strange baby, there was great consternation and a long ride around the country to find the right baby.

After the country became settled, people took turns having dances in their homes. It was a way of meeting neighbours and preventing loneliness. When the weather was cold and the snow deep, they hitched a team of good horses to a sleigh box. Travellers heated rocks and buried them in straw to keep their feet warm and pulled buffalo robes over their laps. During the summer months, they rode saddle horses. One thought nothing of riding a horse twelve miles to a dance, with a good suit of clothes or a dress packed in a gunny sack tied to the saddle.

The fiddle, mouth organ, and accordion ground out such favourites as "The Heel and Toe Polka," "The Log Cabin Jersey," "Rye Waltz," "Marching through Georgia," and "Highland Schottische."

There were no wallflowers in a country with three men to every woman. The men were so anxious to dance that they sometimes tied a handkerchief around one arm, signifying a willingness to be regarded as a lady partner.

Dances lasted all night, partly because the people were young and vibrant, partly because it was safer to wait until dawn to find one's way home across the dark countryside.

≋ CHOCOLATE FUDGE CAKE ≋

This recipe belonged to Mary Stewart, wife of a former member of the North West Mounted Police. After her husband retired from the force, they moved to Leavings, now Granum, Alberta. There she operated a boarding house, which became renowned for its excellent food. The recipe is printed with the permission of Mary Stewart's granddaughter, Mrs. Robert (Jean) Fisher, and comes from a handwritten book that belonged to Mary.

CREAM BUTTER AND sugar together; add eggs and vanilla. Beat well. Sift flour, cocoa, cream of tartar, and salt. Stir into batter alternately with milk. Dissolve baking soda in boiling water and beat into the batter until smooth. Pour into two 8- or 9-inch (20 or 23 cm) well-buttered and floured layer-cake tins. Bake at 300°F (150°C) for 35 to 40 minutes. Cool 10 minutes, loosen, and turn upside down on a wire rack. When cool, frost the layers with chocolate butter icing or caramel icing.

NOTE This cake can also be baked in a 9 × 13 inch (23 × 33 cm) rectangular pan for approximately 45 to 50 minutes.

½ cup (125 mL) butter

1½ cups (375 mL) sugar

2 eggs, beaten

1 tsp (5 mL) vanilla

1¾ cups (450 mL) all-purpose flour

⅓ cup (75 mL) cocoa

1 tsp (5 mL) cream of tartar

½ tsp (2 mL) salt

½ cup (125 mL) milk

1 tsp (5 mL) baking soda

¾ cup (175 mL) boiling water

⚛ JELLY ROLL ⚛

3 eggs, separated

¾ cup (175 mL) sugar

1 tsp (5 mL) vanilla

2 tbsp (30 mL) butter

½ cup (125 mL) water

1 cup (250 mL) flour

1 tsp (5 mL) baking powder

¼ tsp (1 mL) salt

Katie Moffatt brought a jelly roll to a North West Mounted Police Dance at the Regina barracks in 1890. The following recipe is adapted from one in Katie's handwritten cookbook, now in the possession of descendants Mr. and Mrs. William Toole of Calgary, Alberta. This cake may also be baked in two 8-inch (20 cm) round tins and filled as a layer cake.

PREHEAT OVEN TO 400°F (200°C). Line a 15 × 10 inch (39 × 26 cm) jelly-roll pan with waxed paper, grease it well, and sprinkle lightly with flour. Beat egg whites until fluffy. Add sugar gradually and beat until sugar has dissolved and whites stand in peaks. Add egg yolks and beat until thick and creamy. Add vanilla. Heat butter and water (do not boil). Sift flour, baking powder, and salt. Add at one time to the egg-sugar mixture, then fold in lightly. Add all the hot liquid at one time and again fold gently. Spread out in pan. Bake approximately 12 minutes.

While it is hot, invert cake onto a tea towel sprinkled with confectioner's sugar. Cut off hard edges. Spread cake with raspberry jam or lemon butter and roll. Enclose in plastic wrap or waxed paper to keep.

MRS. J.L. SEXSMITH of High River, Alberta, recounted details about her wedding in an interview by E.G. Luxton (Glenbow Archives, 1956):

"When I was a bride, there was no high school or normal [the equivalent of today's teachers' colleges] any nearer than Edmonton, and no business opportunities for young women, so after finishing public school we simply stayed home. We enjoyed many pleasures, however, such as riding, dancing, horseback riding, and swimming in the river. There were no discussions about bath houses or heated pools in those days. Riding sidesaddle over the wide open spaces with thoroughbreds was wonderful. The prairie in spring and summer was covered with long grass, myriad wildflowers. Indeed it was something to be never forgotten!

Mr. and Mrs. Ed Hartt on their wedding day.
GLENBOW ARCHIVES, NC-39-51

"There were not many young women in the district, but there were several bachelors, so my sisters and I had many admirers. I had one in particular, who rode quite a distance to see me as often as he could. Even in cold weather and through deep snow, Lem Sexsmith came to call and always said it was worth it. I was scarcely grown up when my decision was made.

"We had quite a large house and prepared to have the wedding at home, for there was no church in the district. All our friends and neighbours were invited. Miss Janie Suitor, later Mrs. Bob Findley, made my dress, and it took quite a while to make. It was cream cashmere trimmed with cream satin and lace, it had large legs of mutton sleeves, and a long sweeping skirt with a dust ruffle. It was lovely!

On the afternoon of the service one long table was set, and as we did not have enough chairs, we used benches with homemade quilts, which proved quite comfortable. A neighbour, Mrs. Fred Dowell, was an excellent cook and came to help with the preparations. We had a wedding cake, dozens of custard and dried-apple pies, homemade bread and buns, and roast beef. I doubt if there was a turkey in the whole of southern Alberta at the time.

"After the service, we visited, had dinner, and danced until morning. Our music was supplied by Charlie Shattuck and his fiddle, with various guests taking turns on a mouth organ. As there had been a bad storm that night, all the guests stayed until daybreak so they could see to find their way across the unfenced prairie.

"In the morning Lem and I left for our home on the Little Bow, which was the old Samson and Hartford Ranch. We had a good team of horses and a homemade sleigh with blankets and quilts and hot rocks to keep our feet warm. This was our wedding trip, and a wonderful ride it was. To my dismay, several guests followed us and, because of the heavy storm, stayed at our house for a week! What a send-off for a bride!"

A packed snow drift—a path of easy access to a roof top. GLENBOW ARCHIVES, NA-2757-1

★ A RANGELAND SHIVAREE ★

THE CUSTOM OF shivareeing a new bride and groom was observed in many ranching communities. The usual procedure was to gather every noisemaking device the group could find. After the newlyweds' lights went out, the fun-makers surrounded the house, banged pots and pans, rang cowbells, and fired guns until they were invited inside for a party.

Dancing and playing cards and other games would go on until the small hours of the morning. The guests always brought "lunch"— sandwiches, doughnuts, and the makings for coffee. Sometimes the fun-makers got carried away, such as the group of cowboys who decided to surprise their newly married friend, a ringleader of many former pranks.

It was winter when the new husband carried his bride over the threshold of their sod-roofed shack. The couple had just settled down for a good night's rest when the wild group of cowboy friends rode up on their horses and circled the place, whooping, hollering, and firing guns. One of the riders galloped up a packed snowbank and right onto the roof. When the bride and groom looked up, they saw four horse legs protruding through the ceiling above them.

≋ LIGHT FRUITCAKE ≋

This recipe was adapted from the personal cookbook of Mrs. Royden (Jean) Fraser, who got it from her great-aunt, Mrs. Rose Reider. It has been used in western Canada since the turn of the century. It is easy and makes a mild-flavoured fruitcake suitable for weddings, Christmas entertaining, teas, and packed lunches.

SIFT FLOUR, BAKING POWDER, and salt. Cream butter; add sugar and beat until light and fluffy. Add eggs, one at a time, beating well after each addition. Combine dried fruits, almonds, and lemon rind and juice. Fold the dry ingredients alternately with fruit into creamed mixture.

Prepare two deep 8 × 8-inch (20 × 20 cm) fruitcake pans or four 4 × 8-inch (11 × 20 cm) loaf pans. Line pans with brown paper and grease paper well with butter. Pour mixture into pans. Smooth the top of each. Bake at 325°F (160°C) for 15 minutes, then lower temperature to 275°F (140°C). Continue baking for 1½ to 2 hours if using loaf pans, or 2 to 2½ hours if using square pans. Check doneness by inserting a toothpick. If toothpick comes out dry, cake is done.

4 cups (1 L) flour

2 tsp (10 mL) baking powder

1 tsp (5 mL) salt

1 lb (500 g) butter

2 cups (500 mL) sugar

8 eggs

1 lb (500 g) candied citron*

1 lb (500 g) red cherries*

1 lb (500 g) sultana raisins

½ lb (250 g) blanched, chopped almonds

2 lemons, juice and grated rind

* An excellent variation for those who do not care for citron and cherries is to double the amount of sultanas and substitute dried apricots for the cherries. To use apricots, wash and soak for 10 minutes, then chop. Pour ½ cup (125 mL) of Cointreau or brandy over the fruit and leave to soak overnight.

⚜ GINGERBREAD ⚜

2½ cups (625 mL) flour

2 tsp (10 mL) ginger

1 tsp (5 mL) cinnamon

¼ tsp (1 mL) cloves

¼ tsp (1 mL) salt

1 tsp (5 mL) baking soda

1 cup (250 mL) brown sugar

½ cup (125 mL) melted butter
  or margarine

1 cup (250 mL) fancy molasses

2 eggs

1 cup (250 mL) boiling water

Gingerbread can be served as a cake. It is particularly good served warm with sweetened, flavoured whipped cream (see page 93). For an elegant dessert, decorate with slivers of candied ginger.

PREHEAT OVEN TO 350°F (180°C). Sift flour, spices, salt, and soda together. In a large bowl, stir sugar into melted butter or margarine. Add molasses and eggs and beat well. Add dry ingredients alternately with water, beating thoroughly after each addition. Pour into a greased 9 × 13-inch (23 × 33 cm) pan and bake at 350°F (180°C) for 40 to 50 minutes.

⚜ PRESERVED GINGER CAKE ⚜

¾ cup (175 mL) butter

½ cup (125 mL) white sugar

½ cup (125 mL) brown sugar

2 eggs

2 cups (500 mL) all-purpose flour

1 tsp (5 mL) baking soda

½ tsp (2 mL) cinnamon

½ tsp (2 mL) grated nutmeg

½ tsp (2 mL) salt

1 cup (250 mL) sour milk

¾ cup (175 mL) preserved ginger,
  chopped

Ginger was frequently used in drinks, cookies and cake. This recipe makes an attractive and delicious cake to serve with tea or coffee at an evening party or afternoon picnic.

CREAM THE BUTTER until fluffy. Add the sugars, and beat until the brown sugar has dissolved. Beat in the eggs, one at a time. Sift together the dry ingredients. Mix them into the creamed mixture alternately with the sour milk. Fold in the preserved ginger. Spoon into a greased and floured 8-inch (20 cm) tube pan. Bake at 350°F (180°C) for 45 to 50 minutes. Turn out and cool. When almost cool, spread glace icing (see page 92) over the top and let it dribble down the sides.

This prize Hereford bull is proudly displayed at the O'Keefe Ranch near Vernon. THE HISTORIC O'KEEFE RANCH

★ A COWBOY WOULDN'T BE CAUGHT MILKING A COW ★

COWBOYS WERE DEPENDABLE workers, accustomed to danger and discomfort. They willingly rode herd and roped and branded cattle in all types of weather. However, milking a cow was quite another matter.

At that they drew the line, preferring to do without rather than condescend to milking one of the brutes. In one of his papers in the Glenbow Archives in Calgary, John D. Higinbotham recalled that ranchers like Willie Cochrane of the celebrated Cochrane Ranching Company, which ran twenty thousand head of cattle, drove to town and loaded their wagons with cases of condensed milk.

The cows thought no better of the idea. They were range cows, and few of them could be milked without being roped and thrown or run into a narrow chute,

where they were held fast while the hapless milker managed as best he could to secure a few drops of precious liquid.

If the rancher had a wife and children, a little more effort was made. On the Rocking P Ranch it was the Chinese cook who tackled two rangy beasts every night and morning. On the LK Ranch, the job fell to the unlucky person who had not found an excuse to be elsewhere. In C.H. McKinnon's 1979 book *Events of LK Ranch*, former ranch hand Dick Magee recalls, "There were three of the toughest Holstein milk cows that could be found. Most of the men purposefully forgot how to milk after they had a try. When my turn came I always got some but would be exhausted for hours after."

A small rider in a specially constructed basket saddle in front of the Bedingfeld Ranch House, *circa* 1913. A few years later, this ranch was purchased by Edward, Prince of Wales, and became known throughout the world as the E.P. Ranch. GLENBOW ARCHIVES, NA-2467-20

★ LIFE ON A RANCH, 1898 ★

"IT IS TRUE that we do not scatter (visiting) cards or make many afternoon calls, for reasons connected with time and space and other large considerations. We do not give each other dinner parties, but we give each other dinner, generally at 1:00 PM, and beds for the night. People usually come when they have some reason for passing this way; and in ranching country, houses are so few and far between that hospitality of necessity becomes a matter of course. As a matter of course also, people do not expect to be amused. We have no means of formally entertaining each other, and it is not thought amusing to talk from morning till night. A visitor prefers to smoke his pipe in peace, to find his way out and wander round the corrals, inspect any bit of building that may be going on, or cast a critical eye on the stock. After which he saddles his cayuse for himself and departs on his own affairs.

"I like the simplicity, the informality of life, the long hours in the open air. I like riding over the endless prairie, the wind sweeping the grass, the great silent sunshine, the vast skies and the splendid line of the Rockies guarding the West. I like the herds of cattle feeding among the foothills, moving slowly from water to water... I like the clear rivers that come pouring out of the mountains... and the little lakes among the hills where the wild ducks drop down to rest on their flight to the north... I like both the work and the play here... I like the summer and the winter, the monotony and the change. Besides, I like a flannel shirt, and liberty."

From Moira O'Neill's "A Lady's Life on the Ranche," Blackwood's Edinburgh Magazine, Vol. 163, 1898 *(Glenbow Archives)*

⟫ PRINCE OF WALES CAKE ⟪

Edward, Prince of Wales, visited Alberta and purchased the E.P. Ranch in the early 1900s. He must have expressed a liking for spice cakes, because recipes for Prince of Wales Cake appeared in High River cookbooks about that time. This is a traditional raisin spice cake that is moist and delicious.

2 cups (500 mL) raisins
2½ cups (625 mL) water
2 cups (500 mL) brown sugar
1 cup (250 mL) butter or oil
2 eggs
1 tsp (5 mL) vanilla
2¾ cups (675 mL) flour
1 tsp (5 mL) salt
2 tsp (10 mL) baking powder
1 tsp (5 mL) baking soda
2 tsp (10 mL) cinnamon
1 tsp (5 mL) nutmeg

COMBINE RAISINS AND water in a saucepan; simmer for 5 minutes. Cool. Cream butter, sugar, eggs, and vanilla. Add cooled raisin water. In a large bowl, sift together dry ingredients and gradually stir creamed mixture into the dry ingredients. Fold in raisins.

Pour batter into a 9 × 13-inch (23 × 33 cm) greased cake pan. Bake in a 350°F (180°C) oven for 40 minutes or until cake tester comes out clean.

⟫ SHEEP WAGON CAKE ⟪

In the early 1900s, thousands of sheep were pastured on the hills north of Maple Creek, Saskatchewan. They were tended by sheep herders who, from May to October, slept, ate, and carried their belongings in a canvas-covered wagon called a "sheep wagon," Mrs. Irvine Fleming told me in a 1981 interview in Maple Creek, Saskatchewan.

This cake was made by sheep herders and also by cooks at isolated cow camps, as it doesn't require eggs or milk. It is a heavy, tasty cake that keeps well.

1⅓ cups (325 mL) sugar
1½ cups (375 mL) raisins
⅔ cup (150 mL) lard or butter
1 tsp (5 mL) cinnamon
1 tsp (5 mL) nutmeg
½ tsp (2 mL) cloves
1⅓ cups (325 mL) water
1 cup (250 mL) walnuts, chopped
2½ cups (625 mL) flour
1 tsp (5 mL) baking powder
1 tsp (5 mL) baking soda
1 tsp (5 mL) salt

COMBINE THE SUGAR, raisins, lard or butter, cinnamon, nutmeg and cloves in a saucepan with water, and simmer for 10 minutes. Cool. Add the walnuts to the cooled mixture. Mix flour, baking powder, baking soda, and salt, and add to the cooled mixture. Pour into a greased 9 × 13-inch (23 × 33 cm) cake pan or two greased 9 × 5-inch (23 × 13 cm) loaf pans. Bake at 350°F (180°C) for 40-45 minutes or until cake tester comes out clean.

☀ STRAWBERRY SHORTCAKE ☀

2 cups (500 mL) flour

4 tsp (20 mL) baking powder

¼ tsp (1 mL) cream of tartar

¼ tsp (1 mL) salt

½ cup (125 mL) fat (butter or
    shortening)

⅔ cup (150 mL) milk

4 cups (1 L) strawberries

¼ cup (50 mL) sugar

——————

Serves 6

Historically, strawberry shortcake was served when the wild strawberries ripened in the meadows. The shortcake was a rich biscuit dough baked in a round cake pan. The following recipe was taken from Mrs. George Treadway's handwritten recipe book, dated 1898 and now part of the historic collection in the museum at High River, Alberta.

SIFT FLOUR, BAKING powder, cream of tartar, and salt together. Work in fat with your fingers until mixture resembles coarse crumbs. Stir in milk gradually. Place dough on a lightly floured board. Divide into 2 parts and roll each part to fit a round cake pan. Place first layer into lightly greased cake tin. Brush the dough with melted butter, then place second layer over top. Bake at 400°F (200°C) for 20 minutes.

Reserve approximately 12 choice berries for the top. Mash the remaining berries slightly, stir in sugar, and place sweetened berries between the baked layers. Cover the top layer with sweetened, flavoured whipped cream (see page 93) and garnish with whole berries.

Note: The biscuit dough may be rolled and cut into round shapes as for tea biscuits, then split into halves for mini strawberry or peach shortcakes.

★ SPIRIT OF THE WEST ★

THE LETTERS OF Margaret Ward (whose pen name was Mary Inderwick) are stored in the Glenbow Archives. This excerpt is from an 1884 correspondence.

"Think of the delight of this clear air, and let the housekeeper in you think of the appetite which this air gives men and women (though we do not count much in this way here), and the huge meals that must be forthcoming at regular times every day. We have a cow camp and a shack for the cowboys—and they have their own cook so we only get an occasional one for meals if he happens to be riding nearer the house than the camp. They are a nice lot of men. I love their attempt to help me to appear civilized. Though they ride in flannel shirts, they never come to the table in shirt sleeves. There is a black alpaca coat, which hangs in the shack attached to the house, for the cowboys' use, and each one struggles into it to live up to the new regime which began with a bride at the ranche and this is done with such good will that I have no qualms of conscience that I am a nuisance.

"The cowboys back me in all attempts and indeed in all my schemes because I ride well. I verily believe if I did not ride they would have nothing to do with me, as it is, they are rather proud of me...

"I am twenty miles from a woman and though I like all the men and enjoy having them visit I simply long to talk to a woman. About once a month I ride into Saint Francis with Geof and stay a night with my dearest friend Mrs. Milner... It does me good to talk to her, and every man loves her, not in a sighing silly way, but because she always makes them comfortable, darns their clothes and talks to them sternly if they are doing anything wrong. I am sure that she has done more good than two parsons.

"I love the freedom of my life and try to make everyone about me share a bit in my happiness. My life may seem rough and bare, but there is something to compensate one for every hardship and trial. You must come to see me though, for it is the spirit of the west that charms one, and I cannot convey it to you, try as I may. It is a shy, wild spirit and will not leave its native mountains and rolling prairies and though I try to get it into my letters I fail, but I must warn you that if it once charms you it becomes an obsession, and one grows very lonely away from it. No Westerner who has ever felt its fascination ever is really content in the conventional East...

"P.S. Do tell me what the newest hats are like."

Mrs. Sarah Gardiner on Fly. She was an excellent rider and continued to ride sidesaddle long after it was permissible for women to ride regular saddles. MUSEUM OF THE HIGHWOOD.

The substantial house at the Bow Valley Ranch, built by W.R. Hull and later owned by Patrick Burns, *circa* 1895. Charlie Yuen cooked at the ranch for many years before returning to China, where he died soon after. PROVINCIAL ARCHIVES OF ALBERTA, H. POLLARD COLLECTION P307

★ CHARLIE YUEN ★

IN 1980, I spoke with Evelyn and Ed Masse about the Bow Valley Ranch. Evelyn was the ranch manager's daughter, and she shared recollections of Charlie Yuen.

Charlie was proud of his work at the Bow Valley Ranch, and with good reason. The magnificent ranch house was kept clean and tidy. From his kitchen domain came hearty food for the hands and sumptuous meals for the special parties that his employer, Pat Burns, liked to organize. Charlie grew his own vegetables, milked two or three cows, and with the slightest excuse would sneak off on a horse to give a hand to the cowboys.

He made ten to fifteen pies at a time and stacked them up: rhubarb, raisin, dried apricot. It took a week to get to the bottom of that pile. And he made a white cake in such large slabs that the ranch hands nicknamed it "yard cake." Another treat was sugar cookies, four inches in diameter, crisp and fresh from the oven.

Mr. Burns frequently organized hunting parties, and the sportsmen always brought their game back to Charlie, feathers and all, with instructions to hang the dead birds up on the shady side of the house until they nearly fell down. That's when they were supposed to be "ripe" enough. Then they would ask Charlie to cook them. One could hear Charlie swearing and cussing because he had to cook "them birds."

Once, a group of ladies from Calgary decided that they should help Charlie and do the dishes before leaving for home. Poor Charlie knew he was outnumbered. He stood back helplessly while they washed, rinsed, dried, and put the dishes away. Finally, the ladies left, puffed with satisfaction. The minute the last heel went through the door, old Charlie took down every plate, cup, and saucer, washed them again, dried them, and put them back in their proper places.

He was master of his kitchen, and you'd better not interfere.

⋙ YARD CAKE ⋘

This quick, simple recipe makes a cake with an unusual but delicious flavour. Although not Charlie Yuen's original recipe, it comes close to creating the cake described by Evelyn Masse. For a quick family dessert, add broiled coconut topping, or split and put together with raspberry jam. It can also be used as a layer cake, assembled with lemon-butter filling (see page 91) and topped with sweetened, flavoured whipped cream (page 93), or used as a base for trifle.

¾ cup (175 mL) butter or margarine

1½ cups (375 mL) sugar

3 eggs

1½ tsp (7 mL) vanilla

2¾ cups (675 mL) all-purpose flour

1 tbsp (15 mL) baking powder

1 tsp (5 mL) salt

1½ cup (375 mL) milk

PREHEAT OVEN TO 350°F (180°C). Grease and flour two 8-inch (20 cm) round cake pans or a 9 × 13-inch (23 × 33 cm) pan. Cream butter and sugar well. Beat in eggs one at a time; add the vanilla. Sift flour together with the baking powder and salt. Fold in the dry ingredients alternately with milk.

Spread batter in the prepared cake pans. Bake 30 minutes or until cake tester comes out clean. Cool 10 minutes before removing from pan.

⋙ SUGAR COOKIES ⋘

This recipe yields cookies similar to the memorable crisp ones that Charlie Yuen baked at the Bow River Ranch and recalled fondly by the ranch manager's daughter.

1 cup (250 mL) butter

1¼ cups (300 mL) sugar

1 egg

1 tsp (5 mL) vanilla

1 tsp (5 mL) baking soda

1 tsp (5 mL) cream of tartar

½ tsp (2 mL) salt

2½ cups (625 mL) flour

CREAM BUTTER AND sugar. Beat in egg and vanilla. Sift baking soda, cream of tartar, salt, and flour together, then add to creamed mixture. Refrigerate for 2 or 3 hours (or overnight). Roll out on a well-floured board and cut with a round cookie cutter. Bake on a cookie sheet at 375°F (190°C) for approximately 8 minutes (until lightly browned).

☰ GINGER SNAPS ☰

¾ cup (175 mL) margarine

1 cup (250 mL) sugar

1 egg

¼ cup (50 mL) molasses

2 cups (500 mL) flour

1 tsp (5 mL) baking soda

½ tsp (2 mL) salt

1 tbsp (15 mL) ginger

1 tsp (5 mL) cinnamon

¼ tsp (1 mL) cloves

This recipe makes good old-fashioned ginger snaps with a crinkly top. The dough can also be rolled out thinly and cut with a cookie cutter for thin, crisp cookies.

CREAM MARGARINE AND sugar; beat in egg and molasses. Sift dry ingredients together and add to the creamed mixture. Roll the dough into small balls (1 tsp size) and place on greased cookie sheet. Bake at 350°F (180°C). If you like a slightly soft centre, bake for 15 to 20 minutes. For a crisper cookie, bake at least 20 minutes.

CHRISTMAS GINGERBREAD COOKIES

Roll dough out on a lightly floured board, cut with cookie cutter, bake approximately 12 minutes. Frost with butter icing and decorate.

 ★ DANCES OF SODA CREEK ★

EARLY RANCHERS IN the isolated Cariboo country of British Columbia took every opportunity to have some fun. In an article in the winter/spring 1978 issue of *Big Country Cariboo Magazine*, one lonely wife recalled: "One day during winter my husband heard there was to be a dance at Soda Creek. We loved to dance and decided to go. Times were hard. It cost 50 cents to go to a dance so this was a big event for us.

"As we came into town we saw a big barrel with a dipper attached to its rim by an 'S' wire standing right in the middle of the road in front of the hotel. The dipper must have held a pint at least.

"My curious husband went to look. He filled the dipper and tasted the contents. Then I took a drink and it was the nicest tasting stuff. It was rhubarb wine. We found out that old Charlie Ross (a neighbour) placed a barrel there every time there was a dance and it was free to everyone."

PIES, PUDDINGS, ★ AND ★ CRISPS

☰ PIE PASTRY ☰

2 cups (500 mL) all-purpose flour

1 tsp (5 mL) salt

¾ cup (175 mL) cold lard

5 to 7 tbsp (75 to 100 mL) cold water

———————————————

*Makes 2 single-crust pies or 1
double-crust pie*

*During the eighteen years that Sally Smith cooked at the A7 Ranch in
Alberta, she baked four pies almost every day (besides bread, cake, and
muffins). Each ranch hand had his turn choosing the kind of pie to be
made the next day.*

*Flaky pastry for pies and meat toppings was made with home-
rendered lard. Any ranch wife worth her salt could "make up" and "roll
out" half a dozen pies while her bread was in the oven.*

SIFT FLOUR AND salt together. With fingers, work lard into flour until
mixture looks like coarse meal. Sprinkle water on top. Gather dough
together with hands and work into a ball. On a floured board, roll out to
less than ⅛ inch (⅓ cm) thick.

 ★ PRUNE PIE ★

MANY WOMEN WERE totally unprepared for their new lives in the Canadian West. The men on one ranch had longed for a woman's touch
around the place and looked forward to a new bride's arrival with great
anticipation. Her suitcase was hardly unpacked when they urged her to
make a prune pie. Although she had never baked a pie in her life, she
gamely proceeded to work out a method to fit their description of what
a prune pie should be. She prepared a bottom crust, heaped in the dried
prunes (with no presoaking or simmering), covered it all with a top
crust, and baked it for a good long time.

The men on that ranch exemplified the ultimate gallantry, for they
never uttered a word of complaint as they hacked and cut their way
through that pie.

≋ SASKATOON PIE ≋

Berry picking was generally regarded as a task for women and children. During berry season, a rancher's wife tied empty lard pails to the saddle and rode to a stream bank or a dry slope where the saskatoon berries grew. When she returned home, she soaked the berries for an hour or so in lightly salted water to draw out the occasional worm that might otherwise have gone unnoticed.

4 cups (1 L) saskatoons

¼ cup (50 mL) water

2 tbsp (30 mL) lemon juice or vinegar

¼ tsp (1 mL) almond flavouring

¾ cup (175 mL) sugar

3 tbsp (45 mL) flour

¼ tsp (1 mL) salt

PLACE SASKATOONS AND water in a heavy saucepan. Cover and bring to a boil. Turn off the heat and steam for 5 minutes. Add lemon juice and almond flavouring. Mix sugar, flour, and salt; blend with the saskatoons and liquid. Pour into an unbaked pastry shell (see page 78). Cover with pastry top. Make 2 or 3 small slits for steam to escape. Bake in a 400°F (200°C) oven for 35 to 40 minutes or until lightly browned.

Little Katie riding a pig. Animals were very important in the lives of ranch children, who cared for and frequently made pets of them. GLENBOW ARCHIVES, NC-39-302

A cook with four raisin pies ready for baking, *circa* 1880s. The edges have been pressed with a fork to seal the bottom and top crusts together. In early days, pies were baked in a Dutch oven, just like bread. Later, portable stoves with small ovens were carried along at the back of the wagon. GLENBOW ARCHIVES, NA-207-108

WASH RAISINS, ADD WATER, and simmer for approximately 10 minutes. Add brown sugar. Moisten cornstarch with vinegar and orange juice (add a little water if using the chopped orange). Stir into raisin mixture, and cook until thick. Add milk. Roll out half the pie pastry and line an 8-inch (20 cm) pie plate. Fill with raisin mixture. Cover with other half of the rolled pastry. Make 3 to 4 slits in the top crust. Bake at 400°F (200°C) for 35 to 45 minutes.

2½ cups (625 mL) seedless sultana raisins

1½ cups (375 mL) water

¾ cup (175 mL) brown sugar

3 tbsp (45 mL) cornstarch

2 tbsp (30 mL) vinegar

⅓ cup (75 mL) orange juice or 1 orange, chopped (without peel)

1 cup (250 mL) evaporated milk or cream

pastry for a double-crust pie (see page 78)

★ THE SCHOOLHOUSE ★

THE LOCAL SCHOOL was the centre of social life and the locale of box socials, pie socials, picnics, and the annual Christmas concert. Box socials were community dances for which each lady prepared a splendid lunch and packed it into a fancy box. The men bid on the boxes auction style, with the highest bidder winning the box and the right to eat supper with the owner of the box.

Inside the box were slices of chicken, cold ham, or corned beef; fresh homemade buns, sandwiches of potted meat, canned salmon, or egg salad; pickles; generous slices of sponge cake, fruitcake, and mincemeat tarts. White china cups were passed out, and someone carried large enamel pots around the room and filled each cup with coffee or tea.

Pies were a favourite of bachelor cowboys, so for variety the box socials were sometimes replaced by pie socials. Ladies made their specialty—saskatoon, rhubarb, raisin, apple, or custard—and the whole pie was auctioned off to the highest bidder. One pie-hungry cowboy bought three pies, then sat right down and ate them without a pause.

Everyone went to the Christmas concerts. There was an organized program of recitations, plays, and songs, with every child participating. After that Santa Claus bounded in the schoolhouse door and from his gunnysack pack brought out a small gift for each child. Then he passed out candies and oranges to everyone. When the concert was over, the men piled the desks into a corner of the schoolhouse and the fiddler drew out his fiddle for an hour or two of dancing before it was time to go home.

❧ CHRISTMAS PLUM PUDDING ❧

1 cup (250 mL) seedless raisins

1 cup (250 mL) sultana raisins

1 cup (250 mL) currants

⅓ cup (75 mL) brandy, rum, or
　　fruit juice

1 cup (250 mL) grated carrots

1 lemon, juice and rind

¼ cup (50 mL) marmalade or jam

¼ cup (50 mL) walnuts or pecans,
　　chopped

1 cup (250 mL) moist brown sugar

1 cup (250 mL) fine bread crumbs

1 cup (250 mL) flour

1 tsp (5 mL) baking soda

½ tsp (2 mL) salt

1 tsp (5 mL) cinnamon

¼ tsp (1 mL) each cloves, nutmeg,
　　and mace

¾ cup (175 mL) butter (or 1 cup
　　suet)

3 eggs, beaten

_____

Serves 10 to 12

A flaming pudding is a spectacular ending to a festive meal. To flame, heat ¼ cup (50 mL) brandy in a small container. Just before carrying to the table, pour hot brandy over the pudding and set alight.

WASH RAISINS AND currants and place in a large mixing bowl. Add brandy, and if time permits allow fruit to soak for several hours or overnight.

Add carrots, lemon, marmalade, nuts, sugar, and bread crumbs. Sift flour, soda, salt, and spices over the fruit and mix well. Cream butter, and beat in eggs one at a time. Stir into raisin-flour mixture. Spoon batter into a well-buttered 8-cup (2 L) bowl or mould, or into 2 smaller moulds, until ⅔ full. (The mould can be a special pudding mould, salad bowl, metal bowl, Pyrex bowl, a quart (litre) sealer, or empty coffee can.) Cover mould with foil.

Select a lidded pot or kettle large enough to hold the mold. Place a low rack, trivet, or wire on the kettle bottom and set the covered mould on rack. Pour enough water into kettle to reach halfway up the mould. Cover the kettle and bring water to a boil. Maintain steam for approximately 4 hours.

Check periodically during steaming and add more water if necessary. When pudding is done (it is firm and an inserted toothpick comes out clean), remove the foil, let cool, and cover with clean, dry foil. Store in a cool place. The pudding will keep for a long time if kept cool and is best if allowed at least two weeks to "ripen."

Before serving, steam for 1 hour or wrap in foil and reheat for 1 hour in the oven. Unmould on a serving plate and garnish with a sprig of holly. Serve with brown-sugar sauce (see page 93) or hard sauce (see page 84).

⇒ CHRISTMAS CARROT PUDDING ⇐

This recipe makes an excellent, fairly light steamed pudding.

COMBINE CARROTS, POTATO, and butter (or suet). Sift flour, sugar, soda, salt, cinnamon, and nutmeg. Wash raisins and currants. Mix all together and spoon into a greased mould or empty coffee cans until ⅔ full. Cover with 2 layers of foil and tie down with string. Place a metal stand or jar ring on the bottom of a kettle or Dutch oven. Add several inches of water and place the mould on the stand so the water covers ⅓ to ½ of the mould. Cover the kettle and steam for 3 to 4 hours. The pudding will be firm, and a toothpick when inserted will come out clean. When done, unmould, wrap, and store in the refrigerator for 1 to 2 weeks or freeze for longer storage. To reheat, steam for 1 hour or wrap in foil and warm in oven for 1 hour. Serve with brown-sugar sauce (see page 93).

1 cup (250 mL) grated carrots

1 cup (250 mL) grated potatoes

¾ cup (175 mL) butter (or 1 cup suet)

1¼ cups (300 mL) all-purpose flour

¾ cup (175 mL) sugar

1 tsp (5 mL) baking soda

1 tsp (5 mL) salt

1 tsp (5 mL) cinnamon

½ tsp (2 mL) nutmeg

1 cup (250 mL) seeded raisins

1 cup (250 mL) currants

Serves 8

★ PLUM PERFECT ★

TO BRIGHTEN A lonely Christmas, a group of pioneer bachelors planned a get-together to which each bachelor would bring one item for dinner. Jock was to prepare the steamed plum pudding. He followed his mother's recipe, but he had a problem. She had always wrapped the pudding in a clean cloth, and there was no cloth in his shack. After considerable thought, he washed his socks, filled them with pudding, and tied string around the tops. He dropped his pudding-filled socks into a kettle of water and boiled them vigorously for several hours. The pudding was reported to be excellent.

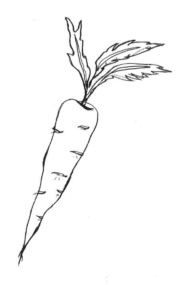

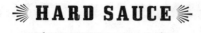

HARD SAUCE

½ cup (125 mL) butter

½ cup (125 mL) fine sugar (berry or
  icing sugar)

1 tbsp (15 mL) brandy

1 tsp (5 mL) finely grated lemon rind

¼ tsp (1 mL) grated nutmeg

Serves 6 to 8

This recipe is less sweet than most hard sauces and is suitable for serving after a heavy dinner.

CREAM BUTTER. Add sugar gradually, continuing to beat until the mixture is light and fluffy. Add the brandy and lemon rind. Beat. Spoon into a glass serving bowl. Grate nutmeg over top. Chill thoroughly.

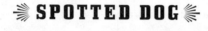

SPOTTED DOG

4 cups (1 L) milk

½ cup (125 mL) short-grain rice

½ cup (125 mL) sugar

½ tsp (2 mL) salt

½ tsp (2 mL) nutmeg

½ tsp (2 mL) cinnamon

1 tsp (5 mL) vanilla

½ cup (125 mL) raisins, washed

Serves 4 to 6

COMBINE ALL INGREDIENTS except the raisins in a 1½-quart (1.5 L) casserole. Bake uncovered at 325°F (160°C) for 2½ hours. Stir in the raisins ½ hour before the pudding is done. Serve with sugar, cinnamon, and milk.

⁂ ORANGE CHARLOTTE ⁂

Oranges and lemons were rare treats, and any desserts incorporating them were given special rating. One of the recipes was a modified version of the classic dessert Orange Charlotte Russe. It was brought to the table in a beautiful china fruit bowl and spooned into sherbet glasses.

SOFTEN THE GELATIN in cold water, add boiling water, and stir until gelatin is dissolved. Add the sugar, lemon juice or liqueur, orange rind and juice. Chill until syrupy. Add egg whites, beaten stiff but not dry. Fold in whipped cream. Pour into a serving bowl and garnish with orange slices. Chill until firm.

4 tsp (20 mL) unflavoured gelatin

⅓ cup (75 mL) cold water

½ cup (125 mL) boiling water

½ cup (125 mL) sugar

¼ cup (50 mL) lemon juice or
   orange-flavoured liqueur

1 tsp (5 mL) grated orange rind

1 cup (250 mL) orange juice and pulp

3 egg whites

1 cup (250 mL) heavy cream,
   whipped

———

Serves 8

Chuckwagon cook Charlie Lehr standing in front of the grub tent during the 1896 High River roundup. He is remembered as one of the best natured and cleanest of the chuckwagon cooks. He never pulled out without seeing that the wagon, harness, and grub were all in order. GLENBOW ARCHIVES, NA-466-22

★ CHUCKWAGON COOKS ★

IT WAS OFTEN said that only a fool argues with a skunk, a mule, or a cook. For those who did, life became unpleasant: the coffee weak, the raisins gritty, and the beans hard.

Although chuckwagon cooks did have a reputation for being cranky, they were resourceful, talented men who worked long hours and had a hard life. They prepared three meals a day with limited ingredients and equipment. They were expert teamsters, capable of driving broncs over rough country, through streams, up steep banks, down hills. It was their job to keep the harness mended and the wagons repaired. Sometimes they acted as "doctor" to ailing cowboys, sewed on buttons, and refereed fights. For these services they received fifty dollars a month.

They could make camp and have a meal cooked in forty-five minutes. As soon as they stopped, they unhitched the chuckwagon horses, unharnessed them and turned them loose, and climbed into the wagon.

They threw out the cook tent, let down the cook's table, put up the cook tent, set the stove in place, put the stovepipe up, and lit a fire. They boiled spuds with their jackets on, put on a pot of pork and beans, fried steaks, boiled some dried apples or prunes, made tea or coffee, and at the proper time called out, "Come 'n' get it before I throw it out."

Chuckwagon cooks achieved their own fame. Ed Larkin made the best raisin pies in the country. Cookie Green served a "duff and dip" for dessert that was talked about long after the roundup was over. "Mulligan Jack" Thomas was appreciated for his sense of humour and his famous dessert "Son-of-a-Gun-in-a-Sack." Charlie Lehr was remembered for his steaks; Billie Grier, for his sourdough. There were Louie Hong, Jack Emsley, Frenchi Ouimet, Dirty Dick, Death on the Trail, Poison Bill Finlay, Willie Andrews, Stone Roberts, and many others—each with his own specialty.

⟫ SON-OF-A-GUN-IN-A-SACK ⟪

When chuckwagon cook "Mulligan Jack" wanted to be especially nice to the "boys" on roundup, he prepared a Son-of-a-Gun. He dropped a clean, smooth stone into the bottom of a sugar sack and made a hoop from a willow branch to hold the top open. He dipped the sack in water and dusted it with flour. Then he spooned in the pudding mixture, removed the hoop, and tied the top. The pudding and sack were immersed in a pail of water and boiled for several hours. When the pudding was cooked, the sack was peeled off and the pudding sliced. Sometimes this pudding was called Duff and Dip; "duff" referred to the pudding, and "dip" to the sauce that was made to spoon over it.

The following recipe has been adapted to ¼ the size usually made by Mulligan Jack.

1¼ cups (300 mL) flour
½ tsp (2 mL) cinnamon
¼ tsp (1 mL) cloves
¼ tsp (1 mL) nutmeg
¼ tsp (1 mL) ginger
½ tsp (2 mL) baking soda
¼ tsp (1 mL) salt
½ cup (125 mL) suet
½ cup (125 mL) raisins
½ cup (125 mL) dates
½ cup (125 mL) milk
½ cup (125 mL) fancy molasses

COMBINE THE DRY ingredients, suet, raisins, and dates in a bowl. Mix to a soft consistency with the milk and molasses. Stir well. Spoon into a bowl until ⅔ full. Cover with foil and secure with a string. Place the bowl on a trivet in a large pot with 2 or 3 inches (5 or 6 cm) of water on the bottom. Cover and steam for 2½ hours. Unmould and serve hot with brown-sugar sauce.

✺ RHUBARB CRISP ✺

FRUIT BASE

4 cups (1 L) rhubarb, cut into
    small pieces

½ cup (125 mL) sugar

1 tbsp (15 mL) flour

¼ tsp (1 mL) cinnamon

CRUMBLY-CRUST TOP

¾ cup (175 mL) brown sugar,
    firmly packed

⅓ cup (75 mL) butter or
    margarine

1 cup (250 mL) flour

1 tsp (5 mL) cinnamon

This dessert is served in early summer.

PLACE RHUBARB PIECES in a 9-inch (23 cm) square or equivalent size casserole. Combine sugar, flour, and cinnamon. Mix with rhubarb.

    Mix the ingredients for crumbly-crust top until the butter resembles coarse crumbs. Sprinkle over rhubarb. Bake at 375°F (190°C) for 30 to 40 minutes or until rhubarb is tender.

★ SHE'S UP TO CHEESE ★

SICKNESS WAS A problem on a lonely ranch. An assortment of home remedies was always kept on hand, in hopes that one would cure the patient and thus spare the long, hard ride to find a doctor. In *Big Hill Country* (Cochrane and Area Historical Society, 1977), a rancher's wife recalled one of her home-nursing experiences:

"One day a frantic neighbour came to fetch me. A lady visitor at his ranch was in great pain, with suspected pleurisy. I was the nearest woman. Would I help? Of course, I rode over and undertook the task of nursing the patient back to health. The neighbour's son helped assemble the ingredients for a mustard plaster and a clean flour sack to put it in. The patient fought like a tiger, but we finally got it on her. Next, I asked for a thermometer. The neighbour's son said they had one and produced a dairy thermometer a foot long and half an inch thick, made of clear glass. We were afraid to put it into her mouth for fear she would bite it off. After some thought it was decided to put it under her arm. I leaned over and held her arm down tight while the young man watched the glass. A full minute passed, then I asked, 'What is her temperature?' He replied, 'She's up to cheese.'

"In spite of us, she recovered and was able to go home the next day. It was just a touch of acute indigestion."

FILLINGS ★ AND ★ TOPPINGS

Mabel Biggs (*circa* 1908) turning her barrel churn by a crank located on the side. After the butter was formed, she would pour in cold water from the nearby well to wash it.

GLENBOW ARCHIVES, NC-43-12

☰ LEMON BUTTER ☰

Lemons were scarce and were treats saved for special occasions.

WASH AND DRY a 16-oz (500 mL) glass jar; keep it warm. Wash and dry lemons; grate rind very finely. Squeeze juice from the lemons. Place lemon rind, juice, butter, eggs, and sugar in a mixing bowl or top of a double boiler. Set saucepan with a small amount of water and simmer on low heat. Stir mixture for 15 to 20 minutes, until it thickens. Do not allow it to boil. Pour into the heated jar. Lemon butter will keep in refrigerator for up to 6 weeks if tightly covered. Serve in baked tart shells or as a filling for jelly roll or yard cake.

2 large lemons (or juice to measure approximately 6 tbsp/100 mL)

1 tsp (5 mL) lemon rind

¼ cup (50 mL) butter

2 large eggs, beaten

1 cup (250 mL) sugar

☰ REGAL CHOCOLATE SAUCE ☰

This is an old recipe from Mary Stewart's handwritten cookbook. It makes a delicious sauce for ice cream, puddings, and cake.

HEAT CHOCOLATE, WATER, and sugar in a heavy saucepan or a double boiler over low heat until the chocolate is melted. Add butter, salt, and vanilla; mix well and simmer for 5 minutes. Beat until smooth. If you prefer a thinner sauce, add water until it reaches the desired consistency.

2 squares unsweetened chocolate

½ cup (125 mL) water

½ cup (125 mL) sugar

1½ tbsp (25 mL) butter

pinch salt

2 tsp (10 mL) vanilla

Makes approximately
¾ cup (175 mL)

≋ CARAMEL ICING ≋

¼ cup (50 mL) butter

1 cup (250 mL) brown sugar

¼ cup (50 mL) milk

1 tsp (5 mL) vanilla

1 to 1½ cups (250-375 mL)

    icing sugar

Makes sufficient to ice a
9 × 13-inch (23 × 33 cm) cake

The flavour of this easy-to-prepare icing tastes very good on chocolate cake and Prince of Wales cake.

MELT THE BUTTER in a heavy saucepan. Add brown sugar and stir over heat for 2 minutes. Add milk and bring to boil. Remove from heat; add vanilla. Cool slightly. Beat in enough icing sugar to make a spreading consistency. Spread on cooled cake.

≋ GLACE ICING ≋
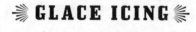

1 cup (250 mL) icing sugar

2 tbsp (30 mL) lemon juice or milk

water to moisten

MIX THE INGREDIENTS together and spread over the top of the cake.

⚛ SWEETENED, FLAVOURED ⚛ WHIPPED CREAM

BEAT THE CREAM until thick. Fold in sugar and vanilla.

½ pint (250 mL) whipping cream

2 tbsp (30 mL) sugar

1 tsp (5 mL) vanilla

⚛ BROWN-SUGAR SAUCE ⚛

MELT THE BUTTER in saucepan; add the brown sugar. Simmer slowly for 2 to 3 minutes, stirring constantly. Stir in the flour. Add hot water and stir. Cook for several minutes. Just before serving, add the vanilla. Serve hot.

6 tbsp (100 mL) butter

1 cup (250 mL) brown sugar

2 tbsp (30 mL) flour

1½ cups (375 mL) hot water

1 tsp (5 mL) vanilla

≋ BROILED COCONUT TOPPING ≋

⅓ cup (75 mL) butter

1 cup (250 mL) coconut (or
    crumbly, crunchy cereal)

1 cup (250 mL) brown sugar

2 tbsp (30 mL) milk

¼ cup (50 mL) nuts

MELT THE BUTTER. Add the coconut (or cereal), brown sugar, milk, and nuts. Mix together and spread over top of cake. Place under broiler until the mixture turns golden. Browning will take only a few minutes, so watch the cake closely.

★ BEVERAGES ★

★ THE FIRST OF JULY ★

IN THE EARLY 1900s the social event of the year was the community picnic on the first of July. There were horse races and horse-breaking events. The children participated in foot races and jumping contests. Married women competed against single women in thread-and-needle races. A tug-of-war pitted the married men against the bachelors. There were wheelbarrow races, egg-and-spoon races, and pie-eating contests.

After the organized events, the children played games of hide-and-seek, ante-I-over, and ring around the rosy. Teams were chosen for ball games. Older men threw horseshoes, and ladies visited.

Two or three families with ice houses and a summer supply of ice brought ice-cream freezers, a block of ice, and the makings for ice cream. The men packed the freezers with chipped ice and turned the handles until they would crank no more. Then they packed them with more ice, covered them with a blanket and left until the ice cream hardened.

When it was time for the picnic lunch, tablecloths and blankets were spread under the trees and the homemade specialties were displayed. Everyone filled a plate with cold baked ham, fried chicken, jellied chicken, potato salad, coleslaw, jellied fruit, chutney, beet pickles, buttered buns, fudge layer cake, sponge cake, ginger cake, jelly roll, rhubarb pie, pumpkin pie and cookies. There was lemonade to drink.

At last the ice cream was unpacked. The thought of its coolness made everyone hurry over with a dish and spoon to stand in line for a taste.

⚛ LEMONADE ⚛

This lemonade concentrate is easy to pack for a community picnic and handy to keep in the refrigerator at home.

SQUEEZE JUICE FROM lemons. Mix all ingredients and leave for 24 hours, then strain and store in a covered jar. To mix, use 2 tablespoons (30 mL) per glass of cold water, or ½ cup (125 mL) per quart (1 L) of cold water, or 2 cups (500 mL) per 4 quarts (4 L) of cold water.

8 lemons
4 tbsp (60 mL) citric acid
2 tbsp (30 mL) tartaric acid
1 tbsp (15 mL) Epsom salts
8 cups (2 L) sugar
rind of 4 lemons
6 cups (1.5 L) boiling water

Picnickers attending a gymkhana on the Roo Dee Ranch, Pincher Creek, Alberta, *circa* 1899. GLENBOW ARCHIVES, NA-184-72

⧽ RHUBARB JUICE ⧼

8 lbs (4 kg) rhubarb

3 quarts (3 L) water

3 cups (750 mL) sugar

Rhubarb, called "the spring tonic," makes a refreshing, attractive summer drink and is a good base for a party punch.

WASH AND CUT rhubarb into small pieces. Add water and simmer slowly until the rhubarb is very soft. Strain to make 1 gallon (4 L) of juice. Cook juice and sugar until boiling. Store in the refrigerator. Serve juice cold. It can also be mixed with equal proportions of 7-Up, ginger ale, or carbonated lemon-lime drink.

★ MOONSHINE ★

THERE WAS A time under the old North-West Territories Act when importing liquor was prohibited. However, a permit entitling the bearer to purchase spirits for sick and domestic purposes could be obtained from the lieutenant-governor. He was kept busy issuing permits twenty-four hours a day.

There was also a great surge in the purchase of food flavourings, particularly Jamaica ginger, which contained not less than 4.5 percent alcohol. Under ordinary circumstances, Jamaica ginger was used as a flavouring, as a laxative, and as a treatment for grippe. After prohibition, it also served as an alcoholic beverage and caused plenty of excitement at various gatherings.

Whisky traders and bootleggers did a flourishing business and kept the police active. Whisky was imported in kegs marked *vinegar*; bags of feed were found with a keg of whisky concealed inside; firkins of butter arrived with a container of liquor covered with butter and a layer of cheesecloth.

Moonshining operations sprang up all over. Blackstrap molasses or a combination of grains and potatoes formed the base of the formula. Barley was turned into beer; fruits, into wine. The scene of one moonshine operation became known as Whisky Coulee and retains the name to this day.

Cowboys at the Turkey Track Ranch near Vanguard, Saskatchewan, having a whisky and poker break inside the corral, *circa* 1914. SASKATCHEWAN ARCHIVES BOARD, R-A2721

★ COWBOY COFFEE ★

THE AROMA OF coffee brought the cowboys hurrying from their bedrolls. The sight of that wide-bottomed, smoke-blackened, five-gallon pot was enough to warm their hearts on even the chilliest morning.

The standard method of making coffee was to place the pot, two-thirds filled with cold water, upon the hot coals to boil. When a rolling boil was reached, the cook dumped the correct amount of coffee on top of the water—1¼ cups of coffee to 1 gallon of water (he measured with his hand). The coffee was brought back to a boil and quickly pulled off to the side and left to steep for a few minutes.

★ QUICK DRAW ★

COWBOYS CAME FROM all over. There were seasoned cowboys from Texas and greenhorns from the British Isles. Young men from eastern Canada came looking for adventure and opportunity. There were characters from the northern states who had crossed the border with tired horses and a price on their heads.

They were men of many talents: farmers, North West Mounted Police officers, artists, musicians, college graduates, poker players, bootleggers. Although they seldom spoke of their past, their place of origin could be determined by their preference for drinking tea or coffee. Outfits operated by men from the British Isles or eastern Canada served tea routinely; among outfits originating south of the border, tea was regarded with disdain, as something akin to poison.

In a 1981 interview with me in Longview, Alberta, Frank Gallup recalled an American-born cowboy named Jim Spratt—a noteworthy character even for a cowboy. One evening when his outfit was camped near a big alkali lake in Saskatchewan, and all the hands were sitting around yarning as usual, Jim stepped up to the stove and lifted the coffee pot to fill up his cup. The cook cautioned, "It's tea; we're out of coffee." Jim pulled out his six-shooter, peppered that pot full of lead, and warned, "You have coffee for breakfast, or you'll get that too."

Coffee was in that pot for breakfast.

≋ BIBLIOGRAPHY ≋

Breen, D.H. *Ranching in the Northwest, 1875-1892.* PhD thesis, University of Alberta, 1972.

Carpenter, Jock. *Fifty Dollar Bride.* Sidney, BC: Gray's Publishing Ltd., 1977.

Cochrane and Area Historical Society. *Big Hill Country: Cochrane and Area.* Cochrane, Alberta: Cochrane and Area Historical Society, 1977.

Douglas, Helen. *Echoes of Willow Creek.* Granum, Alberta: Willow Creek Historical Society, 1965.

Fowke, Edith. *Folklore of Canada.* Toronto: McClelland & Stewart, 1976.

Gould, Ed. *Ranching in Western Country.* Saanichton, BC: Hancock House Publishers, 1978.

Gould, Jan. *Women of British Columbia.* Saanichton, BC: Hancock House Publishers, 1975.

High River Pioneers' and Old Timers' Association. *Leaves from the Medicine Tree.* Lethbridge, Alberta: Herald Printers, 1960.

Higinbotham, J.D. *When the West Was Young.* Toronto: The Ryerson Press, 1933; Lethbridge: The Herald Printers, 1978.

Mather, Ken. *Home Sweet Home: A History of the Historic O'Keefe Ranch 1867-1977.* Vernon, British Columbia: O'Keefe Ranch, 1995.

Ormsby, Margaret A., Ed. *A Pioneer Gentlewoman in British Columbia: The Recollections of Susan Allison.* Vancouver: University of British Columbia Press, 1976.

Pincher Creek Historical Society. *Prairie Grass to Mountain Pass: History of the Pioneers of Pincher Creek and District.* Calgary: D.W. Friesen & Sons Ltd., 1974.

Rutstrum, Calvin. "Sourdough." *The Beaver.* Autumn 1973.

Thomas, G.E.G. *The British Columbia Ranching Frontier, 1858-1896.* MA thesis, University of British Columbia, 1976.

Thomas, Lewis G. *Ranch Houses of the Alberta Foothills.* Paper. Glenbow Archives, Calgary, Alberta, 1974.

Thomas, Lewis G. *The Ranching Period in Southern Alberta,* MA thesis, University of Alberta, 1935.

☀ INDEX ☀

Page references in *italics* refer to photo captions.

duck: Roast Wild Duck, 32
Dutch oven, 10, 20, 23, 47, 48, 55, *80*, 83

Edward, Prince of Wales, 71
Emms, Bessie, 29
E.P. Ranch, *70*, 71

Fenton, Judy Rutledge, 42
Fenton Ranch, 42
fermentation. *See* Sourdough Starter
filling: Lemon Butter, 91
First Nations, and ranching, 1, 32, *46*; and western settlement, 48; and bannock, 55
First of July, 96
Flapjacks, 60
Fort Macleod, 6, *39*, 45, 48,
Fraser, Boyden (Jean), Mrs., 67

Gallup, Frank, 18
gelatin, 29, 85. *See also* Jell-O
ginger, 10, 68, 76, 87; Jamaica ginger, 98; preserved ginger, 68
Gingerbread, 68
Ginger Snaps, 76
Glace Icing, 92
Goddard, Luella, *42*

Hard Sauce, 84
Hawkes, John, 13
High River, AB, 35, 45, 48, 65, 71, 72, *86*
High River Horse Ranch, 39
High River Museum, 58
home remedies, 88
Hopkins, Monica, 30, 50
horseradish: Boiled Beef with Horseradish Sauce, 11;

Horseradish Sauce, 11; Spiced Beef, 26

icing: Caramel Icing, 92; Glace Icing, 92

jam, 58, 64, 75, 82
Jelly Roll, 64
Jell-O, 8. *See also* gelatin
Jones, Charlie, 56

Kells, Edna, 62
ketchup, 16

Lehr, Charlie, 58, *86*
lemon: Lemon Butter, 91; Lemonade, 97
Light Fruitcake, 67
LK Ranch, *40*, 69

Madeira wine, 32
manners and traditions, 35–35, 60, 65, 66. *See also* dances, weddings
Maple Creek, SK, 62
Marinated Onions in Sour Cream, 44
Mass, Evelyn, 75
meat. *See* beef, chicken, duck
Meat Loaf, Ranch House 16
Midway Ranch, *51*
Millarville, AB, 24
Mitford and Cochrane Annual Races, 25
Moffatt, Katie, 64
moonshine, 98
"Mow," *59*
"Mulligan Jack," 54, 87
mustard, 10, 14, 16, 23, 26, 29, 42, 47, 48

mustard sauce, 29

Neutral Hills, AB, *34*
nutmeg, 43, 45, 58, 68, 71, 82, 83, 84, 87
nuts: almonds, 67; pecans, 82; walnuts, 71, 82

O'Keefe, Cornelius and Mary Ann, 28
O'Keefe Ranch, 28, *69*
Okotoks, AB, 25
150 Mile House, BC, 27
O'Neill, Moira, 70
onions: Creamed Onions, 43; Marinated Onions in Sour Cream, 44
Onward Ranch, 26, 27
Orange Charlotte, 85
orange-flavoured liqueur, 85
Osborne, Shirley Merle, 23
Oxley Ranch, 6, 10

pastry. *See* pies
Pickled Beets, 44
pickles/pickling: dill pickles, 42; Pickled Beets, 44; pickled tongue, 29; pickling salt, 12, 14, 29, 42; pickling spice, 12, 29
Pie Pastry, 78
pies: Beefsteak and Kidney Pie, 10; Prune Pie, 78; Raisin Pie, 81; Saskatoon Pie, 79
pork: and beans, 86; bacon, 48, 60; pork chops, 38; pork sausages, 40; salt pork, 1, 48, 59; salt-pork fat, 55
Potluck Bean Supper, 47
poultry. *See* chicken, duck

BEULAH (BUNNY) BARSS holds a home economics degree from the University of Saskatchewan and an MA from the University of Calgary and qualified as a dietitian at the Royal Victoria Hospital in Montreal. She is dedicated to preserving the rich heritage of ranching and pioneering experiences, particularly regarding food and cooking. She lives in Calgary, Alberta.